PRAISE FOR *CREATING URGENCY*

"In a world where most marketing dollars get wasted on noise, Steven Kahan shows how to focus on what really drives growth—creating urgency that moves buyers to act. This is a must-read for every SaaS founder and GTM leader."

—Michael Triplett, Managing Director, Insight Partners

"*Creating Urgency* shows marketers how to turn compelling ideas into action that moves the needle, from message to accelerating revenue growth. Steve maps the journey with practical plays any team can run tomorrow."

—Casey Cheshire, Founder, Ringmaster Conversational Marketing

"Steve has distilled decades of go-to-market experience into a powerful, practical guide. *Creating Urgency* turns the art of influencing buyer behavior into a repeatable science backed by data and execution discipline."

—Josiah Sternfeld, CEO, Integrous Analytics

"Few marketers truly understand how to connect storytelling, data, and urgency into a motion that drives revenue. *Creating Urgency* lays out that blueprint. It's the ultimate guide for leaders who want to accelerate results."

—Damon Tompkins, CEO, Pathlock

"*Creating Urgency* shows how to turn complex products into must-have solutions by making invisible problems impossible to ignore. Steve's frameworks have helped companies like ours grow faster and market smarter."

—Simon Azzopardi, CEO, CoreView

"Every company faces the same challenge: how to make buyers buy now. *Creating Urgency* gives leaders the playbook to do exactly that, turning hesitation into decisive action and momentum into growth."

—James Legg, Start-Up Executive and Former CEO, Thycotic

"*Creating Urgency* gets to the core of efficient growth: aligning product, marketing, and sales around moments that compel buyers to act. Steve translates hard-won operating experience into clear frameworks that leaders can put to work immediately."

—Thomas Krane, Managing Director, Insight Partners

CREATING URGENCY

ALSO BY STEVEN MARK KAHAN

Be A Startup Superstar
High-Velocity Digital Marketing

CREATING URGENCY

How to Flip the Script—and Win

STEVEN MARK KAHAN

MATT HOLT

Matt Holt Books
An Imprint of BenBella Books, Inc.
Dallas, TX

This book is designed to provide accurate and authoritative information about B2B sales and marketing. Neither the author nor the publisher is engaged in rendering legal, accounting, or other professional services by publishing this book. If any such assistance is required, the services of qualified professionals should be sought. The author and publisher will not be responsible for any liability, loss, or risk incurred as a result of the use and application of any information contained in this book.

Matt Holt is an imprint of BenBella Books, Inc.
BenBella Books, Inc.
8080 N. Central Expressway
Suite 1700
Dallas, TX 75206
benbellabooks.com
Send feedback to feedback@benbellabooks.com

Matt Holt and *BenBella* are federally registered trademarks.

Printed in the United States of America
10 9 8 7 6 5 4 3 2 1

Library of Congress Control Number: 2026011128
ISBN 9781637749807 (hardcover)
ISBN 9781637749814 (electronic)

Copyediting by James Fraleigh
Proofreading by Michael Fedison and Natalie Roth
Text design and composition by Aaron Edmiston
Cover design by Morgan Carr
Printed by Lake Book Manufacturing

To my wife, Terry—
Your love, strength, and belief in me have made everything possible.
This book, like everything I've built, is for you.

To my children—Jennifer, Chris, Ryder, and Jackie—
You inspire me every day with your heart, drive, and character.

To my grandchildren—Hunter and Savannah—
May you always chase what matters, with urgency and joy.

To my business colleagues—
Thank you for your trust, your grit, and your shared pursuit of greatness.
This journey wouldn't have been possible without you.

CONTENTS

Introduction

WHY YOU HAVE TO CREATE URGENCY NOW

You didn't pick up this book because you're bored. You picked it up because something's not moving fast enough—pipeline, decisions, momentum, buyers.

Let's be honest: Right now, you're under more pressure than ever.

More pressure to deliver leads.

More pressure to close deals.

More pressure to show ROI—not in quarters, but in weeks.

And all while your team is asked to do more with less.

You're chasing buyers who go dark.

You're watching great products stall in "Maybe later."

You're staring at a pipeline that looks full . . . until it doesn't convert.

And no matter how hard you push, things aren't moving.

Here's the truth most won't say out loud: *You're not losing to your competitors. You're losing to inertia.*

You're losing to buyers who are overwhelmed, distracted, and playing it safe.

They don't say no. They just . . . disappear. And by the time they wake up, your deal is gone.

Why?

Because what you're offering doesn't feel urgent.

Not yet.

Not to them.

But it's not your fault.

You were trained to explain value. To differentiate. To follow up. What no one taught you was how to make a buyer feel the pain of doing nothing.

That's what this book is for.

In this market—where budgets are tight, cycles are long, and noise is everywhere—urgency isn't a tactic. It's a survival skill.

Companies don't miss their number because they have a bad product. They miss it because they're solving a problem that doesn't feel urgent.

In B2B, people don't buy "should-haves." They buy "must-haves." And the only way to become a must-have is to show buyers what it's costing them to wait.

This book will show you how. It's built from the trenches—from the seven high-growth companies I helped grow, my years of leading go-to-market (GTM) teams, and the battle-tested lessons behind my first book, *High-Velocity Digital Marketing*.

Inside, you'll get:

- Real frameworks I've used to accelerate pipeline and make the buyer move now.
- Examples of how to flip the script on stalled deals.
- Tools and checklists to make urgency operational, not accidental.
- Plays that don't just create engagement—they create movement.

This isn't a theory book. It's a manual. Because in today's economy, movement isn't automatic.

You have to make it happen.

If you're tired of waiting for buyers to act—and ready to start making them move—this book is for you.

Let's go.

Chapter 1

THE BOILING FROG EFFECT

If you drop a frog in boiling water, it jumps out immediately. But if you put it in cool water and slowly turn up the heat, it stays until it boils alive.

It's a metaphor so vivid, it's become cliché—yet it perfectly explains why so many buyers fail to act until it's too late.

In business, problems often emerge gradually. A misconfiguration here. A duplicated process there. A slow buildup of risk, inefficiency, or missed opportunity. Leaders and teams adjust, compensate, absorb—until suddenly, they're cooked.

As marketing and sales leaders, this is one of our biggest challenges: Buyers don't see the threat until they're already deep in it. Our job? Make them feel the heat now—before it's too late.

WHY BUYERS STAY IN THE WATER

Most organizations aren't ignoring problems because they're reckless. They're ignoring them because:

- The pain builds slowly.
- The problem has become normalized.
- It doesn't seem urgent—yet.

Think of a company using spreadsheets to manage compliance workflows. It's clunky, but "it works." Then one day they fail an audit, and suddenly they're scrambling. Or consider a security team that's tolerated shadow IT (the use of technology, software, or services within an organization without official IT approval or oversight) for years—until a breach exposes everything.

This is the Boiling Frog Effect in action. And inaction isn't apathy. It's invisibility.

This phenomenon doesn't just apply to internal operations—it affects entire markets. Categories stagnate. Buyers settle for "good enough" tools because they don't feel the cost of staying still. As a result, breakthrough solutions fail to break through. It's not because the offering is weak. It's because the status quo hasn't yet become uncomfortable enough to abandon. Your job is to make them uncomfortable—with precision and credibility.

YOUR JOB IS TO TURN UP THE HEAT

To create urgency, you must break the comfort of the warm water. That means you can't just sell features or future benefits. You have to make the current state feel unacceptable.

Here's how you can do it like the great marketers have.

Expose Hidden Problems

Use assessments, audits, or simple tools to reveal what buyers can't see. It's not about telling them they have a problem. It's about showing them.

Example: A cybersecurity company offers a free misconfiguration scan. The buyer thinks their environment is secure—until the scan shows admin access is open to 120-plus inactive users. The heat just turned up.

Quantify the Consequences of Waiting

Don't just talk about ROI. Put a price on doing nothing.

Example: A facilities platform tells buyers, "Our solution can save you $30K/year." Nice. But it's more powerful to say, "Every month you wait is costing you $2,500 in energy waste. We can show you how to fix that."

Now the heat isn't abstract. It's on a timer.

Use Contrast and Before/After Framing

Make the current state look bad by comparison.

Example: "Right now, your onboarding process takes 9 days. Here's how one client cut that to 36 hours—and doubled offer acceptances."

The buyer can't unsee that. And now, they want out of the hot water.

TURN COMPLACENCY INTO DISCOMFORT

What makes the Boiling Frog Effect so dangerous is that it doesn't trigger urgency until the damage is irreversible. So, your job is to bring discomfort forward in time. Turn passive awareness into active tension.

That doesn't mean fearmongering. It means:

- Using data to tell uncomfortable truths.
- Showing what happens if nothing changes.
- Using real examples that feel uncomfortably familiar.

It's one thing to say, "Manual processes are inefficient." It's another to say, "We just worked with a company like yours. They thought things were fine—until a $700K client walked because onboarding took too long."

Now that's heat.

REAL-WORLD EXAMPLE: IT OPERATIONS

A software-as-a-service (SaaS) company selling observability tools ran into a common wall from their prospects: "We already have monitoring." So instead of pitching more features, they created a free "Noise Index" diagnostic that showed how much alert noise teams were drowning in.

Most buyers were shocked. One team discovered 87% of their alerts had no actionable resolution. They weren't just boiling—they were vaporizing.

Urgency exploded. Why? They didn't know the water was that hot.

THE EMOTIONAL TIPPING POINT

Buyers may be aware of a nagging problem, but unless that awareness is paired with emotional tension—embarrassment, fear of loss, reputational risk—they'll stay still. Your messaging must introduce a moment of emotional confrontation:

- "If your CFO saw this report, what would they ask?"
- "If your competitor launched this next week, how would you respond?"
- "If your board asked why your implementation is stuck at 70%, what's your answer?"

Questions like these convert passive pain into urgency. And urgency leads to movement.

Also, don't underestimate the power of internal politics and inertia. Sometimes, you need to equip your champion with not just logic, but language. Give them the phrases, stats, and visuals that help them argue for change inside their company. Make the invisible boiling water impossible to ignore, even for stakeholders further removed from the pain.

SHOW THE BOILING POINT BEFORE IT HITS

The best urgency-driven marketing doesn't exaggerate the threat. It reveals it. It accelerates the moment of clarity. It helps buyers realize they're in trouble before they actually are.

You're not creating a false emergency. You're showing them the real one—just faster. And that's how you get them to jump.

Action Checklist

- ☐ Identify one problem your buyer is "living with" that's slowly compounding.
- ☐ Create a simple tool, scan, or diagnostic to expose it.
- ☐ Quantify the monthly or annual cost of doing nothing.
- ☐ Use before/after framing to dramatize contrast.
- ☐ Make the current state feel unacceptable—not just improvable.

Chapter 2

THE MOMENT OF REALIZATION

Every great marketing story has a turning point—that split second where the buyer sees something they can't unsee. A realization that breaks through the noise and flips the switch from "Maybe later" to "We need this now."

This is the moment of realization.

It's not about showing them what you do. It's about showing them something about themselves. Something they hadn't noticed, or hadn't admitted, until now.

As a sales and marketing leader, your job is to create this moment on purpose.

WHAT IT FEELS LIKE

Great realization moments are:

- *Emotional*: They trigger discomfort, surprise, or even embarrassment.
- *Personal*: They reflect the buyer's own situation, not just a generic industry trend.
- *Irreversible*: Once the buyer sees it, they can't go back to pretending it's not a problem.

Think about when someone shows you a slow leak in your roof, a hidden security risk in your environment, or a data point that changes your entire strategy. It's not just helpful—it's jolting. And once that light turns on, urgency follows.

REALIZATION ≠ EDUCATION

Education is helpful. Realization is transformative.

Most marketing stays at the "educate the market" level:

- Here's a stat.
- Here's a trend.
- Here's how our product works.

That's fine—but it doesn't spark action. What does? A mirror. Your goal is to reflect the buyer's current blind spot back at them in a way that feels both familiar and urgent.

And don't underestimate how rare—and powerful—this moment is. In a world of banner blindness, inbox clutter, and executive overwhelm, grabbing attention is hard. Holding it is harder. What creates breakthrough isn't louder messaging—it's a flash of self-recognition. When buyers see something they've overlooked or underestimated, especially if it's costing them money or exposing them to risk, it stops the scroll. It gets meetings. It starts conversations that matter.

HOW TO ENGINEER THE "AHA!" MOMENT

Use Personalization to Hit Close to Home

Generic insights don't create breakthroughs. Personalized insights do.

Example: Instead of saying, "75% of companies overspend on SaaS," you run a quick scan with a license optimization tool and say, "You're paying for 432 unused licenses. That's $108,000/year."

That's not a stat. That's a gut punch.

Leverage Contrast to Make the Gap Obvious

Realization often comes from seeing the difference between now and next.

Example: Your recruitment platform shows buyers a side-by-side benchmark. You tell a prospect, "Your offer acceptance rate is 42%. Top performers in your industry average 79%." The buyer suddenly sees what they're missing—and what it's costing them.

Create Emotional Tension with Storytelling

Data can wake people up. But stories move them.

Example: A healthcare IT company told the story of a similar-sized hospital that delayed upgrading its patient intake system. The result? A three-month backlog, a PR crisis, and a $1.2M loss in billables. It wasn't a scare tactic. It was a true story that mirrored their reality.

That story caused more pipeline movement than any feature launch.

Name the Problem—but Make It About Them

It's not enough to name the problem. You have to make it *their* problem.

Example: "You don't have a CRM problem. You have a follow-up accountability gap. Leads are sitting in limbo for 13 days. Want proof?" Then you show it. Now it's not just about features. It's about failure they can see.

Layer in Stakes and Timing

To maximize the impact of the realization, tie it to timing. If a buyer believes the problem can wait, they will wait. Your job is to compress that timeline by linking the realization to a deadline or an approaching consequence. What are the real costs of waiting? What's at risk this quarter, this month, or before their next board meeting?

Example: "We've seen teams in your position get hit with audit penalties because they didn't fix this by fiscal close. That's 27 days from now." Now it's not just a problem—it's a ticking clock.

Also, help them visualize the snowball effect. Most pain points start small but grow quickly. If your buyer understands that what feels like an annoyance now will become a crisis later, you've reframed the threat. And reframing is what sparks movement.

DELIVERING THE MOMENT

This moment of realization can come in many forms:

- A diagnostic or benchmark
- A story about a peer or competitor
- A visual comparison (before/after, side-by-side)
- A statement that breaks through denial

But whatever the format, it must hit them with truth + relevance + tension. Otherwise, it's just more noise.

REAL-WORLD EXAMPLE: ENTERPRISE FINANCE

A forecasting software vendor struggled to get CFOs to engage beyond surface demos. Their pitch was technically solid, but it lacked spark. So, they created a "Projection Precision Score" that scanned the buyer's Excel forecasting model and returned a score out of 100.

Most execs scored under 60. But more importantly—they were surprised. They'd trusted their models. Now they didn't.

The result? A 3× increase in demo-to-pipeline conversion. Not because the tool changed. But because the buyer had a moment of realization that their current approach wasn't just flawed—it was dangerous.

YOU'RE NOT JUST MARKETING A PRODUCT; YOU'RE REVEALING A TRUTH

The best marketing doesn't sell something new. It reveals something true. And when buyers realize that truth—when they feel it, not just hear it—they move. They reprioritize. They find budget. They escalate the conversation. They realize that staying the same is no longer an option.

Action Checklist

- ☐ Identify the single insight that will shift your buyer's mindset.
- ☐ Create a personalized way to deliver that insight (scan, benchmark, story).
- ☐ Use contrast to show what they're missing compared to best-in-class.
- ☐ Frame your insight around them—not just the industry.
- ☐ Practice storytelling that makes the problem real, not abstract.

Chapter 3

THE COST OF INACTION

Most marketing focuses on what buyers gain if they act.

But smart sales and marketing professionals know the real driver of urgency isn't upside—it's loss.

That's why great marketing doesn't just talk about what you'll get. It shows what you're already losing. What you'll continue to lose. And what it will cost you if you wait even one more quarter to act.

Because when the cost of doing nothing becomes clear—action follows.

WHY BUYERS DEFAULT TO INACTION

Inertia is the real competition in most sales cycles. It feels safe. Familiar. Budget-friendly. And above all, it feels like a neutral choice.

But it's not.

Doing nothing is *never* free. It's not neutral. It's often the most expensive decision of all. The problem is most buyers don't see it that way—unless you show them.

WHY SHOWING ROI ISN'T ENOUGH

You might think the antidote to inaction is ROI. And while ROI is useful, it's not usually enough to spark urgency. Why? Because ROI is *hypothetical.* Future-focused. "If you buy this, here's what might happen."

That's helpful—but safe. What's *urgent* is when a buyer sees what staying put is already costing them. Not later. Now.

And that window is narrower than ever. With sales cycles lengthening and CFOs scrutinizing every line item, the only deals getting approved are those tied to clearly defined business risks or losses. If the impact of doing nothing isn't obvious, the proposal never makes it to the top of the stack—or worse, it never leaves the inbox. The burden of proof isn't just to show value—it's to show pain. Now.

HOW TO SHOW THE REAL COST OF DOING NOTHING

Put a Price Tag on the Status Quo

The current way of doing things has a hidden cost. Make it visible.

Example: A scheduling optimization company doesn't say, "We'll help you improve utilization." Instead, they say, "Your current setup is costing you $132,000/month in idle technician time. That's $1.5M/year—and rising."

Suddenly, doing nothing looks a lot more expensive.

Break Down the Cost into Bite-Size Hits

Annual numbers feel abstract. Monthly, weekly, or daily costs feel real.

Example: "Every day your reps spend manually inputting CRM notes is costing $4,300 in lost productivity. That's $21,500 a week—just walking out the door."

That's a jolt. And jolts move buyers.

Tell a True Story of "Delay → Damage"

Data convinces. But stories compel.

Example: A compliance automation company shares the story of a firm that delayed switching systems. Why? "We're not ready." Then they failed an audit, got fined $500K, and lost a key client who saw the news. When the story ends with "they became a customer two weeks later," buyers listen.

Use Side-by-Side Comparisons

Nothing sharpens urgency like contrast.

Example:

	Staying the Same	Making the Switch
Manual processing costs	$412K/year	$43K/year
Customer churn rate	17%	8%
SLA compliance	66%	98%

When the difference is visual, the choice becomes obvious.

Use Time as a Weapon

Delay is rarely framed in terms of loss—but it should be.

Example: "If you wait 90 days to implement, you'll lose $75K. That's not opinion. That's math."

Now the buyer has to justify waiting. Most can't.

REAL-WORLD EXAMPLE: RETAIL INVENTORY MANAGEMENT

A SaaS company helping retailers optimize stock levels used to lead with features: "Predictive demand modeling, AI-driven replenishment." It landed—sometimes.

Then they revised their pitch to start like this:

"Last year, you had 29% of your inventory go unsold. That cost you $3.1M—not including storage and disposal."

And suddenly, the conversation wasn't about features. It was about survival. That company's win rate jumped 43%—not because their product got better, but because their buyers saw what inaction was already doing to them.

WHAT HAPPENS WHEN THE COST BECOMES REAL

When buyers understand the cost of inaction, they:

- Escalate internally faster.
- Look for budget they didn't think they had.
- Move their solution from "nice-to-have" to "need-to-have."

They don't just want ROI. They want to *stop the bleeding.* That's the power of showing what it costs to wait.

Action Checklist

- ☐ Calculate the monthly or quarterly loss caused by the status quo.
- ☐ Frame those numbers in real-world terms (time, revenue, risk).
- ☐ Create a story of a delayed decision that led to loss.
- ☐ Use visuals or side-by-side comparisons to dramatize the cost.
- ☐ Make the buyer defend delay—instead of you defending urgency.

Chapter 4

MAKING THE INVISIBLE, VISIBLE

Most buyers don't fix problems they can't see.

They're not lazy. They're not incompetent. They're busy: flooded with noise and overwhelmed by decisions. Unless a problem is screaming at them—or already on fire—it stays in the shadows.

But here's the truth—the most urgent problems are often invisible:

- Misconfigured security settings
- Slow process bleeds that compound over time
- Opportunity costs buried in "how we've always done it"
- Risk hiding in fragmented workflows, unused licenses, or outdated systems

Your job as a sales and marketing leader? Shine a spotlight on what they're missing. Turn what's hidden into something they can't ignore.

WHY INVISIBILITY IS THE ENEMY OF URGENCY

People don't act on abstract risk. They act on revealed vulnerability.

Think about a health checkup. If your doctor says, "You're probably fine, but let's keep an eye on things," you don't change your habits. But if the blood work comes back with a clear warning—"You're prediabetic"—suddenly your diet, exercise, and sleep all become top of mind. That's the power of visibility. Buyers are the same. The moment they see the issue in their own data, environment, or process—that's when change begins.

And that moment of visibility is your best shot at earning urgency. Most sales cycles don't stall because buyers don't care—they stall because buyers don't know. They don't know what they're missing, what it's costing them, or what risks they're quietly accumulating. When you reveal it—clearly, credibly, and without judgment—you trigger motion. Visibility makes the problem real. And what's real gets budgeted.

HOW TO REVEAL WHAT'S BEEN HIDDEN

Use Diagnostics to Uncover the Unseen

Don't tell the buyer they have a problem. Show them their data—and let them discover it themselves.

Example: A Microsoft 365 governance platform offers a free scan showing which users have excessive permissions, shared folders exposed to the public internet, and misconfigured multifactor authentication (MFA) policies. The scan takes five minutes. The results? Often shocking.

That's not a product pitch. That's a flashlight in a dark room.

Turn Internal Pain into External Insight

Sometimes the buyer knows there's a problem, but hasn't been able to name it.

Example: A DevOps company offers a "Time to Resolution Assessment." It breaks down incidents by category and time spent. The buyer sees that 64% of Priority 1 (P1) incidents are caused by a recurring misconfiguration in the Continuous Integration/Continuous Delivery pipeline. They'd suspected it. Now it's confirmed. And that confirmation creates urgency.

Use Benchmarks to Reveal the Gap

Sometimes buyers don't know what "good" looks like, so they assume their current state is fine.

Example: A content marketing platform runs a benchmark that says: "You publish 1.4 posts per week. Companies in your category publish 3.6. Your average page view is 298; top performers average 1,200."

Now the gap is visible. And so is the opportunity cost. Benchmarks aren't just about comparison. They're about provoking movement.

Don't Just Describe the Problem—Visualize It

A picture changes everything. If you can turn data into a heat map, dashboard, or visual gap analysis, you take a conceptual issue and make it *real.*

Example: A financial controls platform shows buyers a heat map of access rights by department. One team glows red—14 users with admin rights, 11 of whom haven't logged in for 90+ days. No one has to interpret that. It screams risk.

That heat map creates urgency—faster than 10 slides ever could.

STORIES THAT SPARK VISIBILITY

One SaaS company working with midsized manufacturers offered a "Quote Velocity Audit." It showed how long it took from customer inquiry to quote approval. In one case, the buyer saw they were taking 6.8 days—while competitors averaged less than 24 hours.

They had no idea. But once they saw the dashboard, the conversation shifted from "Maybe next quarter" to "Can we pilot this next week?"

Another example: A customer experience platform used to lead with features—omnichannel tracking, sentiment analytics, and so on. Good stuff. But what moved the needle was their "Silent Churn Detector." It showed how many customers hadn't been contacted in 90+ days and had no support tickets or logins.

One buyer saw over 2,300 customers flagged. That was over $2M in at-risk revenue. They signed within a month.

MAKING THE PROBLEM REAL—WITHOUT SHAMING THE BUYER

There's a fine line between urgency and shame.

You want the buyer to feel exposed—not attacked. Surprised—not humiliated.

That's why your visibility tools should lead with:

- *Neutral language*: "Here's what we found," not "Here's what you screwed up."
- *Reassurance*: "Most companies we scan have similar issues."
- *Empowerment*: "Here's how you can fix it—fast."

This positions you as a partner, not a critic. You're not scolding them. You're guiding them.

VISIBILITY CREATES OWNERSHIP

When a buyer can see the problem—in their own world, with their own data—they feel something new: *responsibility*.

Before, the risk was hypothetical. Now it's personal. Before, the inefficiency was abstract. Now it's visualized. Before, the opportunity loss was theoretical. Now it's measured. And once they own the problem, they start looking for a solution.

Action Checklist

- ☐ Identify the top one or two problems your buyer likely doesn't realize they have.
- ☐ Create a free scan, audit, or benchmark to surface those issues.
- ☐ Use visuals to make the problem unmissable (heat map, chart, graph).
- ☐ Deliver insights in a neutral, constructive tone—not accusatory.
- ☐ Frame visibility as empowerment: "Now you can act."

Chapter 5

THE X-RAY EFFECT

Imagine walking into a doctor's office with a vague pain in your leg. The doctor pokes around, shrugs, and says, "Take some ibuprofen. Should be fine."

Now imagine a different experience: They take an X-ray. And there it is—a clear fracture. Not only do you know what's wrong, but you also see it.

Which version drives action?

That's the difference between generic marketing and X-ray marketing. Generic marketing says, "You probably have a problem—we can help." X-ray marketing says, "Here's *your* problem. Right here. This is why it hurts." When buyers can see the issue—clearly, unmistakably—they don't need convincing. They need a plan.

THE POWER OF VISUAL DIAGNOSIS

The X-ray works because it:

- Proves the problem exists.
- Localizes the pain.
- Removes ambiguity.
- Provides confidence in the path forward.

That's what great marketing should do. And in complex B2B buying journeys, this is especially powerful. Most buyers aren't resisting because they're skeptical—they're hesitating because they can't *see* the issue clearly enough to justify a decision. Your job is to remove that fog.

This isn't about flashy visuals—it's about targeted, undeniable proof. Today's buyer is skeptical of claims, cautious with budgets, and buried in vendor noise. They don't want another pitch deck. They want clarity. If you can provide a window into their current state—rooted in data, surfaced in context, and delivered with credibility—you become a partner, not a peddler. The best X-ray tools don't push a product. They pull the truth to the surface.

WHAT THE X-RAY EFFECT LOOKS LIKE IN MARKETING

Personalized Audits or Scans

A generic report is like a WebMD article. A personalized scan is like an X-ray with your name on it.

Example: A privilege access management solution doesn't just say, "Many organizations have excessive access permissions." It scans the buyer's Active Directory and shows them that 61% of users have admin-level access. The scan doesn't just identify risk—it reveals where it lives.

Suddenly, the buyer has clarity. And urgency.

Benchmark Comparisons

Another part of the X-ray effect is *context*. You're not just revealing the issue—you're showing how it compares to healthy standards.

Example: An applicant tracking system includes a "Hiring Funnel Efficiency Score." The buyer sees their time-to-hire is 39 days. The benchmark? Twenty-one. Now you've shown it's not just slow—you've *proven* it's inefficient.

Just as an X-ray shows a fracture compared to the healthy bone, benchmarks provide contrast. And contrast creates movement.

Layered Visibility

The best X-rays go deeper than surface-level symptoms. In marketing, that means revealing not just *what's broken*, but *why it's broken*—and what's at stake if it stays that way.

Example: A cloud cost optimization platform offers a tiered report:

- Tier 1: Wasted spend
- Tier 2: Root causes (idle workloads, misaligned instance types)
- Tier 3: Recommendations and projected savings

That layered insight transforms the conversation from "Should we?" to "How soon can we start?"

MAKING THE INVISIBLE URGENT: THE THYCOTIC PLAYBOOK

When I joined Thycotic as chief marketing officer, we were at a pivotal crossroads. Insight Venture Partners had just invested. We were sitting at $6 million in revenue, and sales had flatlined. The company had a solid product that protected privileged passwords across operating systems, databases, networks, and applications. But the market wasn't responding.

Why?

Because nobody felt the urgency to buy.

How Thycotic Created Urgency

Step 1: Amplify the Analysts

We began by leveraging analyst research to legitimize the problem. Forrester released a report stating that 80% of all security incidents were due to weak or stolen passwords. We amplified this insight across every channel—on our website, in sales presentations, in social and traditional media, and with our partners. This created third-party urgency that prospects couldn't ignore, because it wasn't just Thycotic saying it—it was a trusted industry authority.

Step 2: Create Personal Urgency with Free Tools

To make the problem personal, we developed a highly valuable free tool: the Password Discovery Tool. This feature, originally part of our paid product, uncovered every privileged password within an organization. By giving it away, prospects could suddenly see the scale of their vulnerabilities. Nothing drives urgency like staring at hundreds—or even thousands—of unmanaged privileged credentials in your environment. It transformed an abstract concern into a visible, undeniable risk.

Step 3: Create Market Urgency with Proprietary Research

We expanded urgency creation by commissioning and publishing the annual State of Privileged Password Management report. This global study exposed the widespread and dangerous state of password mismanagement. The data fueled webinars, podcasts, social media, and media coverage—arming our sales team and partners with powerful stories. Prospects now saw not only their personal risks but also how they compared with the broader market, making the issue impossible to ignore.

Step 4: Create Measurable Personal Urgency with Self-Assessments

Next, we launched the Privileged Password Security Benchmark, an interactive self-assessment tool that graded organizations from A to F on their security practices. We personalized follow-ups by geography, size, and industry—showing prospects how their scores compared to peers. This created measurable urgency by giving IT leaders proof that they were falling behind, and ammunition to justify purchases internally.

Step 5: Align Internal Champions with Influencers

Finally, we created the Privileged Password Policy Template, mapping security best practices to regulations. This aligned CISOs (who cared about regulatory compliance) with IT administrators (who controlled budgets and daily operations). The tool gave both audiences a common language and framework, helping internal champions make the case for Thycotic more effectively.

The Results

This five-step system for creating urgency became the foundation of Thycotic's growth. Over the next several years, the company hit its number 23 quarters in a row, scaling from $6M to $140M in revenue. In 2021, Thycotic exited for $1.4B. The lesson: Urgency creation isn't just a sales tactic; it's a growth engine.

Making the Invisible, Visible

1 **Amplified the Analysts**
Amplified a report that 80% of all security incidents were due to weak or stolen passwords.

2 **Created Personal Urgency**
Offered free Password Discovery tools that uncovered privileged passwords and exposed vulnerabilities.

3 **Created Market Urgency**
Published State of Privileged Password Management reports with proprietary data, showing industry-wide risks and benchmarks.

4 **Made Personal Urgency Measurable**
Launched the Privileged Password Security Benchmark, a grading system (A–F) allowing IT professionals to see their security posture and compare it to peers.

5 **Linked Internal Champions with Influencers**
Built templates for buyers unsure how to create access rules, aligning best practices and compliance with daily operations, providing immediate value.

These tools transformed invisible risks into visible, measurable problems that required immediate action.

THE PSYCHOLOGY BEHIND IT

When buyers are shown something they didn't know—but instantly recognize as true—it builds trust. Fast.

That's the magic of the X-ray effect:

- It removes ambiguity.
- It delivers proof, not persuasion.
- It makes the invisible visible (without hype).
- It replaces "Trust me" with "See for yourself."

And once someone sees it, they can't unsee it.

BUILDING YOUR X-RAY TOOL

You don't need to develop a full-blown SaaS platform to create this effect. X-rays can be delivered in many ways:

- A short intake form with a customized output
- A PDF scorecard
- A spreadsheet-based audit
- An automated scan (if your product allows it)
- A benchmark report with dynamic data

The format isn't what matters. What matters is that it shows their reality, in a way they haven't seen before.

X-RAY WITHOUT OVERWHELM

One mistake some companies make is trying to show *too much*. Remember: A good X-ray doesn't need to be exhaustive—it needs to be *diagnostic*. Show the two or three things that matter most. Make them real, relevant, and visual. Let the buyer draw the conclusion. When they say, "Wow, I didn't know this," you've done your job.

Action Checklist

- ☐ Identify the #1 invisible problem your buyer has, but doesn't see.
- ☐ Build a tool or a scan that reveals it in their environment.
- ☐ Include benchmark or comparative context to show the gap.
- ☐ Deliver the results in a way that's visual, personal, and easy to share.
- ☐ Let the insight speak louder than your pitch—and invite the conversation from there.

Chapter 6

CREATING CONTRAST

Most buyers don't make decisions in a vacuum—they make them in comparison.

They compare:

- Now vs. later.
- Current vs. possible.
- Known vs. unknown.
- You vs. the status quo.

This is where the power of *contrast* comes into play. It's one of the most underused—and most effective—techniques in urgency-driven marketing. If the status quo feels "good enough," your job isn't just to prove your solution is better. It's to *make the current state feel clearly worse*. When you sharpen the contrast, you shift perception. And perception—not logic—is what triggers action.

WHY CONTRAST DRIVES MOVEMENT

Imagine two emails in your inbox.

Email A:
"Our software improves collaboration across teams."

Nice. But vague.

Email B:
"Your team spends 4.2 hours per week chasing updates. One of our clients cut that to 45 minutes—in 3 weeks."

Now you're picturing the gap. And once you see the gap, you want to cross it.

That's the essence of contrast. It frames your offer in a way that *magnifies the pain of staying the same*—and amplifies the appeal of acting now.

THE SCIENCE OF PERCEIVED VALUE

In behavioral psychology, people are more likely to act when they can *clearly compare options*, rather than evaluate one in isolation.

This is called *relative valuation*—and it's why before/after stories, side-by-side visuals, and competitor comparisons work so well. Buyers want to feel the difference. Not just read about it.

If you describe your solution in isolation, it might sound nice. If you describe it *next to the painful reality of what they're doing now,* it suddenly feels necessary.

That's why contrast isn't just a messaging technique—it's a revenue catalyst. The human brain is wired to evaluate by difference. If you fail to supply that difference, buyers won't act—not because they disagree, but because they can't see the urgency. Your job is to control the frame: Frame the current state as risky, inefficient, or wasteful, and your solution as the clear leap forward. This isn't embellishment—it's making truth visible by comparison.

THREE FORMS OF CONTRAST THAT CREATE URGENCY

Before and After

This is the classic transformation format. Show the buyer what life looks like before using your product—and what it looks like after.

Example:

Before

- Spreadsheets
- Manual approvals
- Four-day average response time
- Three people involved in every task

After

- Automated workflows
- Instant approvals
- Same-day turnaround
- One-touch resolution

It's not about bragging. It's about *making the pain of the present look ridiculous.*

With Versus Without

This is a simple, punchy framework for showing contrast without needing deep transformation.

Example:

Without Us

- 22% drop-off during onboarding
- Manual, error-prone data entry
- Nine days to go-live

With Us

- 6% drop-off
- API-connected sync
- 48 hours to go-live

The human brain understands side-by-side comparison faster than abstract storytelling. It forces a decision point.

Now Versus If You Wait

This one is powerful for time-sensitive decisions. Instead of focusing on transformation, focus on *decay*.

Example: "If you wait 6 months to implement this system, you'll burn through $330,000 in overtime—and still be behind your competitors."

It's not about fear. It's about focus.

REAL-WORLD EXAMPLE: DATA ANALYTICS

A data visualization platform wasn't breaking through in finance teams. Too many dashboards, not enough impact. So, they created a campaign around "What your CFO sees today vs. what they *could* be seeing."

The visual was simple:

- Left side: Spreadsheet dump, red rows, outdated graphs
- Right side: Trend-line insights, real-time alerts, margin forecasts

The messaging?

"Your CFO isn't ignoring your insights. They can't *see* them."

Meetings spiked. Demos accelerated. Why?

The contrast made the pain visible.

Tactics to Create Sharper Contrast

- *Use screenshots*: Show side-by-side workflows. Visuals drive urgency faster than copy.
- *Benchmark against industry standards*: "Your churn rate is 18%. Best-in-class is 7%." Let them feel the gap.
- *Use metaphors*: "Managing your compliance manually is like balancing your books in a notebook." Simplicity increases punch.
- *Pull from their world*: If your ideal customer profile is warehouse managers, show actual pallet scans. If they're sales leaders, show CRM data snapshots.
- *Use relatable time frames*: "Every week you wait, you're losing 14 hours of productivity." Tied to their calendar. Not a concept.

WHY CONTRAST WORKS BETTER THAN FEATURES

Features tell. Contrast shows.

Buyers don't want to be sold to. They want clarity. Contrast gives them a lens to see the difference for themselves. And once they see it, they want to be on the right side of the picture.

TURNING FREE TOOLS INTO REVENUE ENGINES

One of the most powerful ways to create urgency and contrast isn't to explain the problem—it's to let your buyers discover it for themselves.

That's exactly what free tools can do when built with intent. They expose hidden risks, make problems personal, and turn passive observers into high-intent prospects. Free tools are not giveaways. They are strategic X-rays that surface issues your buyers didn't know they had—or had buried under a pile of competing priorities. The key is this: They don't just deliver value. They deliver clarity. Let's break down how to do it right.

Start with a Problem Worth Revealing

Your free tool must zero in on a problem that's real, urgent, and invisible. Something your market vaguely knows exists but can't quantify.

Don't try to showcase your product's breadth. Focus instead on revealing one painful gap. One costly blind spot. Whether it's unmonitored privileged access, shadow cloud assets, misconfigurations, or compliance violations—give your buyer a window into what they can't currently see.

Make the Discovery Emotional and Measurable

When your free tool delivers results, make those results feel personal:

- Expose how many risks or gaps exist.
- Assign a score, grade, or benchmark.
- Map the problem to a financial or regulatory impact.

Your goal is to take a vague "We should probably fix that someday" and transform it into "We need to fix this now."

Don't Just Reveal—Prescribe

The best free tools don't just say "you have a problem." They offer a path forward. Include a personalized report that:

- Summarizes the findings.
- Explains the risks.
- Recommends best practices.
- Shows how your full product solves the issue continuously.

That's the bridge between free and paid. The value is clear—but the long-term solution lives in the full platform.

Make the Follow-Up Feel Like Help, Not a Pitch

Once someone downloads or engages with your tool, don't send them into a generic drip sequence. Train your sales reps to say things like:

"Hey, I saw you ran the scan—what grade did you get?"

"Would you like help walking through the results?"

"Want to see how your peers in the industry compare?"

This reframes your outreach from a pitch to a consult. It builds trust. And it invites the buyer to reengage with a sense of ownership over the problem.

Free tools, when done right, are urgency accelerators. They don't wait for the buyer to connect the dots. They do the work for them. They show the buyer the problem. They make it measurable. They give them the language to justify change. And they make acting now feel smarter than waiting.

In a world where your biggest competitor is indifference, nothing cuts through like a tool that proves the threat is already inside the house—and you just helped them see it. That's how urgency gets created—and how revenue follows.

Action Checklist

- ☐ Build a simple "Before/After" story for your top three use cases.
- ☐ Create a visual side-by-side comparison: now vs. future state.
- ☐ Use time-based contrast to show what happens if they wait.
- ☐ Use free tools to expose the painful now and desirable after.
- ☐ Don't describe the better future—show how bad it is without you.

Chapter 7

FUTURE-BACK STORYTELLING

Most B2B sales and marketing starts with the present.

- "Here's what your team is dealing with."
- "Here's how our product solves it."
- "Here's the ROI you can expect."

That's fine—but it's not how visionary decisions are made. When buyers only think forward from the present, they're anchored in limitations:

- Budgets
- Politics
- Bandwidth
- Fear of failure

But when they think from the *future back*, everything changes. They start with a bold vision of what they *want* to become—then reverse engineer how to get there. That's *future-back storytelling*. And it's how you break through when logic isn't enough.

WHAT IS FUTURE-BACK STORYTELLING?

Future-back storytelling starts by painting a compelling vision of a better reality—one that the buyer deeply wants but hasn't yet figured out how to reach. Instead of anchoring to today's pain, you anchor to *tomorrow's potential.*

You then help the buyer realize:

1. That future is possible.
2. Others are already getting there.
3. Their current approach won't cut it.
4. You can help them build the bridge.

It's not a pitch. It's an awakening.

WHY IT WORKS

In high-consideration B2B decisions, buyers aren't just solving problems—they're trying to create outcomes:

- Launch new products
- Win new markets
- Retain top talent
- Operate with less risk
- Shift from reactive to strategic

When you tell stories that start *from* those outcomes—and map the journey backward—buyers listen. You're not interrupting their thinking. You're giving it form.

Take the example of talent acquisition. Imagine you're selling recruitment software. The typical pitch:

- You're losing candidates.
- Interviews are delayed.
- Offer acceptance is low.
- We fix that.

But now imagine a future-back story:

"Imagine a hiring experience where you post a job Monday, get auto-shortlists by Tuesday, schedule interviews with one click, and have a signed offer by Friday. Your hiring managers love it. Your candidates rave about it. You've reduced time-to-hire by 60% and kept every key role filled for the last two quarters. That's what your peers at [Company X] are doing. Here's how they got there—and why you can too."

That's not a product pitch. That's *a future the buyer wants to live in*. And once they picture that future, they start asking, "What's stopping us from doing this now?"

Future-back storytelling isn't just about inspiring the buyer—it's about disarming the internal resistance that slows down deals. When you anchor a conversation in the present, every objection becomes a roadblock: budget, timing, competing priorities. But when you anchor in the future, those objections shift. The question becomes: *"What's our plan to get there?"* That mindset reframing changes the internal dialogue inside the buyer's organization. Instead of debating the validity of your solution, they start aligning around the need to move forward. It creates internal champions because the story isn't about you—it's about where they want to go. And your job is to make the path visible, believable, and actionable.

ELEMENTS OF A POWERFUL FUTURE-BACK STORY

Lead with the Vision

Open with a vivid description of what's possible—not what's broken.

Example: "Imagine a security environment where every misconfiguration is auto-remediated within 60 seconds. Audits take hours, not weeks. And your board dashboard is real time, risk ranked, and built for decisions."

The buyer leans in, not because they're in pain—but because they see what they're missing.

Show Proof of Life

Future visions can feel like vapor—unless you ground them in real examples.

Example: "One of our customers—a global logistics firm—implemented this model last year. They've cut their breach exposure window by 88%, and their chief information security officer now runs quarterly security strategy sessions instead of daily fire drills."

This makes the future real—and reachable.

Show the Path in Reverse

The future-back path doesn't just say, "Here's what to do." It says, "Here's how others got there—starting where you are."

Break it down in phases:

- Phase 1: Visibility (e.g., run the diagnostic)
- Phase 2: Remediation (e.g., fix the top 10 issues)
- Phase 3: Automation (e.g., enforce controls)
- Phase 4: Strategic Ops (e.g., shift from fixing to forecasting)

This roadmap becomes a blueprint for the buyer's next 90 days. And it makes the leap feel manageable.

Make the Future Feel Inevitable

Your story isn't just about what could happen. It's about what *will* happen—with or without the buyer.

Example:

"In 18 months, most of your peers will be operating this way. Budgets are shifting. Expectations are rising.

"The only question is: Will you be ahead of that curve—or catching up?"

That's not pressure. That's perspective. And it works.

REAL-WORLD EXAMPLE: AIOPS PLATFORM

An enterprise AIOps vendor stopped leading with "mean time to resolution" metrics and started leading with this:

"Imagine an environment where 90% of incidents are resolved before they impact users—and your operations team becomes a strategic force for uptime."

They followed that with a story of a company that moved from 14 manual workflows to one predictive engine. In six months, their SLA compliance jumped from 72% to 98%. The final slide wasn't a demo. It was a visual timeline of the transformation—starting with a two-week pilot. Buyers stopped asking, "Why now?" and started asking, "What's step one?"

WHEN TO USE FUTURE-BACK VS. PRESENT-FORWARD

Scenario	Use Present-Forward	Use Future-Back
Buyer is in crisis	✓	✗
Buyer is unaware of problem	✓	✗
Buyer is forward-thinking	✗	✓
Buyer is stuck in "maybe later"	✗	✓
Buyer has a goal but no roadmap	✗	✓

If the buyer is in pain, start with the problem. If the buyer is stuck or passive, show them what could be—and why they don't want to miss it.

FUTURE-BACK MARKETING = VISION + BELIEVABILITY

You can't fake this. The future you describe has to:

- Be *emotionally desirable.*
- Be *credible based on your product and others' results.*
- Be *mapped in a way that makes taking the first step obvious.*

Done right, it's not fantasy. It's a call to action rooted in possibility—and backed by proof.

Action Checklist

- ☐ Identify the outcome your buyer most wants but doesn't yet have.
- ☐ Craft a vivid, emotionally desirable picture of that future.
- ☐ Use customer stories or peer examples to make it real.
- ☐ Build a roadmap from future to present—not the other way around.
- ☐ Show that the future is already arriving—and the only question is timing.

Chapter 8

URGENCY ANCHORED IN TIME

If there's one thing every great deal needs, it's a deadline. Without a clock, buyers drift. They say:

- "Let's revisit this next quarter."
- "We need to align stakeholders."
- "Let me get through budget season first."

But time kills deals. Every day that passes without urgency is a day closer to the status quo winning. That's why elite marketers don't just tell compelling stories—they tie them to the calendar. They turn time into tension. And they anchor urgency in moments that matter.

WHY TIME CREATES ACTION

Psychologists call it temporal discounting: the tendency for people to prefer immediate rewards over future ones. We all do it. We'll procrastinate what's good for us tomorrow if there's no pressure today.

But flip that logic—and time becomes your secret weapon. When the consequences of waiting are made real, or when a meaningful deadline appears, people stop browsing. They start acting.

Sales and marketing that anchors urgency in time does two things:

1. It creates *momentum* ("This must happen now").
2. It creates *decisiveness* ("This opportunity will pass").

Without time? Your message is just a nice idea. With time? It becomes a priority.

THE PROBLEM WITH OPEN-ENDED MESSAGING

Too many B2B campaigns are open loops:

- "Our platform helps you drive better results."
- "We offer a free trial."
- "Let's talk when you're ready."

But "when you're ready" almost never arrives. There's always another meeting. Another quarter. Another fire to put out. That's why urgency tied to *something happening soon*—a deadline, a shift, a date, a trend—can change the game. It gives buyers a reason to act *now*, not later.

SIX WAYS TO ANCHOR URGENCY IN TIME

Use Upcoming Industry or Regulatory Deadlines

If your buyer's industry is facing a compliance change, audit requirement, or policy deadline—*use it.*

Example: A data privacy platform ran a campaign leading into General Data Protection Regulation's (GDPR) enforcement date.

The message?

"You have 38 days left to comply. We'll get you ready in 21."

Meetings surged. Pipeline accelerated. No one wanted to get caught unprepared. Deadlines that already exist in your buyer's world are powerful tools. Tie your product directly to the cost of not being ready.

Link to Budget and Planning Cycles

Buyers often plan purchases quarterly or annually. If you know when their planning window opens or closes, aim there.

Example: A cloud platform targeted CFOs during October–November, when many teams were finalizing their budgets for the following year.

Subject line:

"Still budgeting for Q1? Don't miss the infrastructure savings window."

They didn't just pitch savings. They pitched *timing*—and that changed everything.

Leverage Internal Time Pressures

What's happening in your buyer's business right now?

- New product launches
- Seasonal ramp-ups
- End-of-quarter hiring blitzes
- M&A integrations
- Expansion plans

These moments come with urgency—and pressure to get things done *fast*.

Example: A scheduling automation tool found that retail chains scramble to onboard seasonal employees every November. So, in October, their campaign hit inboxes:

"Still using spreadsheets to schedule Black Friday coverage? Let's fix that before it costs you customers."

It wasn't just a clever line. It was a timely trigger.

Create Your Own Deadlines

If none exist, invent one. Urgency doesn't require global shifts. It just needs relevance and a real time constraint.

Ways to do this:

- Limited time offers
- Campaigns that expire
- Enrollment windows
- "Fast track" programs that close soon
- Free trial that must be activated by X date

Example: A cybersecurity vendor offered a "Free Threat Exposure Report—available only through April 30." The report was automated. But the deadline created urgency. Buyers didn't want to miss it—and conversions jumped.

Highlight the Accumulating Cost of Delay

When time passes without action, something is usually being lost: money, efficiency, opportunity, or talent.

Put a number on it.

Example: "Every month you delay onboarding automation, you're losing $43,000 in recruiter hours and 17 top candidates to faster-moving competitors."

Now waiting feels *expensive*. Even if buyers don't feel pain yet, you can show them what's eroding silently—and how quickly it adds up.

Forecast the Near Future (Then Own It)

If you can project what's about to change in their world—and get there before anyone else—you own the urgency.

Example: A vendor in the AI observability space ran a "June 2024 Readiness" campaign around anticipated Microsoft Azure model changes.

The message?

"These changes will affect 100% of GenAI workloads. You need to adjust policies now—or risk data drift at scale." Buyers didn't know it yet. But once they saw what was coming, they moved.

REAL-WORLD CASE: HR TECH CAMPAIGN WITH TIME ANCHORING

A high-volume recruiting platform launched a campaign in mid-January. They'd previously been vague: "We help you hire faster."

This time, they tied the message to *timing*:

"March is the highest candidate drop-off month of the year."

"You have 30 days to fix your funnel before it costs you Q2 revenue. We'll deploy in 7."

That shift—from generic value to time-bound action—lifted response rates by 41% and doubled demo-to-opportunity conversions. It worked because the buyer didn't just see value. They saw a *clock* ticking toward loss.

URGENCY ≠ PRESSURE

There's a difference between urgency and aggression.

- Urgency is *contextual.* It's based on truth.
- Pressure is *tactical.* It's based on fear or manipulation.

Anchoring urgency in time isn't about false scarcity or gimmicks. It's about showing why *now* matters more than "someday."

When done well, it sounds like:

- "The window to stay ahead is closing."
- "Others are already adjusting—are you?"
- "This only becomes harder [or more expensive] the longer you wait."

Time becomes a truth-teller. And urgency becomes aligned with leadership—not desperation.

TIME, URGENCY, AND THE EXECUTIVE MINDSET

Here's the secret most marketers forget:

Executives think in timelines.

Quarters. Roadmaps. Planning cycles. Fiscal years. If your offer doesn't fit into their calendar logic, it gets sidelined. But if you anchor your story to their time map—you get on the agenda. Every CMO, CRO, or CIO wants to make strategic bets *before* their window closes. Show them the window. Then help them jump through it.

Urgency without timing is just noise—but urgency aligned to strategic timing becomes a force multiplier. The most successful revenue leaders I've worked with don't just generate demand—they engineer timing. They study fiscal calendars, product roadmaps, buying-committee cycles, and even board meeting schedules to strike at the moment when movement is most likely. Urgency becomes unstoppable when it collides with executive intention and internal momentum. That's why time-based messaging isn't just good marketing—it's disciplined GTM strategy.

Action Checklist

- ☐ Identify one or two real deadlines already in your buyer's world (compliance, budget, product launches).
- ☐ Use those moments to tie urgency to real consequences.
- ☐ If no deadline exists, create one—and give it weight.
- ☐ Quantify the monthly or quarterly cost of delay.
- ☐ Show that the earlier they act, the bigger the win—and the easier the change.

Chapter 9

THE THREAT OF IRRELEVANCE

In B2B sales and marketing, we often frame the threat as risk:

- Risk of security breaches
- Risk of compliance failure
- Risk of inefficiency, delay, or churn

But in fast-moving industries, there's a deeper, more existential threat: *irrelevance.* Not catastrophic failure. Not dramatic collapse.

Just . . . fading out. For instance:

- Being too slow to keep up
- Being left off buyer shortlists
- Watching competitors leap ahead
- Still "working on it" while others are innovating

And here's the catch: *Irrelevance doesn't feel urgent—until it's too late.* That's why it's your job as a marketer to surface this quiet danger and make it unignorable. Not with scare tactics—but with clarity, contrast, and truth.

THE SLOW FADE

Most companies don't die from a single, explosive failure. They die from staying comfortable too long:

- Processes that worked fine last year but are now dragging results
- Tools that technically function, but no longer compete
- Teams that are efficient but not evolving

You don't need to show buyers that they're broken. You need to show them that *they're falling behind*—and fast. Because here's the uncomfortable truth: The world is changing faster than most businesses are evolving. And no one wants to be the last one using yesterday's playbook.

WHY IRRELEVANCE WORKS AS A MARKETING TRIGGER

Unlike fear-based urgency (which can backfire), irrelevance hits in a different place—*in status, reputation, and ambition.* No CMO wants to tell the board, "We're now behind our peers." No IT leader wants to admit, "We missed the AI wave." No CEO wants to hear, "We're not even in the conversation." That's why, when you frame the buyer's current path as increasingly out of step with the future, you get attention. You're not attacking them. You're warning them—and offering a way to reenter the race.

SIGNS OF IRRELEVANCE THAT BUYERS MISS

Your marketing should surface signals that scream:

- "You're drifting out of alignment."
- "The market has shifted without you."
- "Your peers are gaining ground."

Examples of early indicators:

- Declining engagement or Net Promoter Scores
- Longer sales cycles (because messaging isn't resonating)
- More manual work while competitors automate
- Falling behind industry benchmarks
- Inability to integrate with modern stacks
- Stale branding or dated user interface/user experience (UI/UX)
- Fewer request for proposal (RFP) invitations or analyst mentions

Each of these is a whisper of irrelevance. Your job is to make it heard loud and clear.

TACTICS TO SURFACE THE THREAT OF IRRELEVANCE

Benchmark Performance Publicly and Privately

Give buyers a way to see how they stack up—even if it stings.

Example: A marketing automation platform built a "Relevance Score" based on deliverability, personalization, and automation. When buyers ran the assessment and got a 42/100, it wasn't scary—it was embarrassing. And embarrassment moves people.

Benchmarks aren't just for optimization. They're mirrors. And sometimes, what buyers see shocks them into motion.

Compare Buyer's Tech Stack to the Market Leaders

Reframe the conversation:

It's not about what your tool *does*—it's about how your tool helps buyers catch up.

Example: "We analyzed 50 high-growth SaaS companies. Eighty-two percent use automated onboarding workflows. You're still sending PDFs and follow-up emails manually. That gap isn't just inefficient—it's making you look behind."

Now you're not selling features. You're selling relevance.

Use Social Proof That Signals the Shift Has Already Happened

"Be the first" isn't always powerful. But "Don't be last" is.

Example: "In the last 90 days, 24 companies in your sector switched to real-time financial reporting. What used to be 'leading-edge' is now standard."

This flips the buyer's psychology from curiosity to urgency. They don't want to be the laggard.

Reveal the Opportunity Cost of Staying Traditional

Traditional tools and approaches aren't just outdated—they're expensive in what they *fail to enable.*

Example: "Legacy IT workflows delay innovation cycles by 6–12 months. That means your competitors are launching twice as fast. Every quarter you delay modernization, you give away market share—quietly."

That's the threat of irrelevance: not visible loss, but invisible opportunity given away.

Use Future-Back Language (from Chapter 7)

Don't just say "you're falling behind."

Say, "Here's what the next 12–18 months will look like for companies that evolve—and what it will feel like if you don't."

Example messaging:

"Soon, your buyers will expect a real-time dashboard, not a weekly update.

"Your candidates will expect offers within 48 hours—not 9 days.

"Your competitors will build AI copilots—while your team still runs reports manually."

Paint the future. Then ask:

"Are you prepared to compete in that world?"

REAL-WORLD EXAMPLE: EMAIL SECURITY

An email security vendor shifted their messaging from "Stop threats" to "Stay relevant in the new threat landscape."

They showed how attackers were using large language models to craft phishing attempts with AI, and how traditional spam filters were failing. The pivot wasn't "You'll get hacked." It was:

"You're using filters designed for 2016 threats—in a 2026 environment."

That story didn't scare people into buying. It showed them they were becoming irrelevant without knowing it. Conversions went up. Sales cycles shortened. Because buyers *hate* the idea of being left behind.

MAKING IRRELEVANCE PERSONAL, NOT ABSTRACT

Irrelevance works best when it's tied to:

- A person's role ("Your peers are already presenting these insights to the board").
- A buyer's brand ("Your product experience doesn't reflect your innovation goals").
- A company's positioning ("Your messaging no longer resonates with modern buyers").

Don't talk about irrelevance *in general.* Make it *their* problem. One they can fix—but only if they act now.

WHY THIS WORKS IN EXECUTIVE CONVERSATIONS

Executives aren't scared of problems. They're scared of stagnation. They want to be proactive. Cutting-edge. Forward-looking. So, when you show that their current tools, processes, or strategies are quietly aging—they move. Not because you scared them. But because you activated their ambition.

The fear of irrelevance may be quiet, but it's deeply personal—and universally felt by high performers. In my experience, the best campaigns tap into that latent anxiety not by sounding alarms but by shining lights. When you show executives what's changing, what their peers are already doing, and how small gaps today become major disadvantages tomorrow, they listen. Not because they're afraid to fail—but because they refuse to be forgotten. Irrelevance isn't about being wrong. It's about being late. And that makes it one of the most powerful urgency drivers in modern B2B marketing.

Action Checklist

- ☐ Identify where your buyer is quietly falling behind (tech, process, speed, messaging).
- ☐ Use benchmarks or competitive insights to make that gap visible.
- ☐ Frame the threat as "losing relevance," not just "facing risk."
- ☐ Ground it in their world—their role, their brand, their outcomes.
- ☐ Offer a clear way to reestablish relevance—and become a leader again.

Chapter 10

THE BUDGET IS THERE—IF THE URGENCY IS REAL

Sales leaders hear it all the time:

"It's not in the budget."

"We're out of funding for this quarter."

"Maybe next fiscal year."

It's the most common excuse for stalled deals—and the most misunderstood.

Because here's the truth:

Budget is almost never the real problem. It's a reflection of something deeper: *priority.* If your solution solves a top-priority problem, the budget appears. If it doesn't feel urgent? You'll be pushed to next quarter. Or next year. Or never. So, if you want to win more deals, don't just make a case for value—*create a case for urgency that justifies immediate investment.*

THE GREAT BUDGET MYTH

When a buyer says, "We don't have the budget," what they're really saying is:

- "We're not sure this is important enough."
- "We don't want to go to bat for this right now."
- "We have other fires to put out."
- "We're not emotionally invested yet."

In other words: *We're not convinced this matters more than everything else on our plate.* That's not about money. That's about mindset. And your job as a sales and marketing leader is to shift it.

BUDGETS ARE FLEXIBLE—FOR THE RIGHT PROBLEMS

Let's be real: Companies find money when they want to.

- When a top customer is at risk, budget shows up.
- When Legal says, "We need to fix this," the funds are unlocked.
- When the board demands results, priorities shift.

If your offer feels urgent, strategic, or politically important—budget will be found.

If it feels like a "nice-to-have"? You're toast. This is why marketers must not just talk about *value*—they must *prioritize the pain*. When the pain is real enough, the budget isn't an obstacle. It's a formality.

The secret most top-performing sales and marketing teams know? Urgency doesn't just unlock budget—it justifies leadership. When buyers feel pressure from above to show progress, hit targets, or solve nagging inefficiencies, they don't need a bigger budget—they need a more defensible decision. That's why urgency that's anchored in strategic objectives doesn't just get you into the budget. It gets you sponsored by leadership. In today's environment, the deals that get funded aren't the cheapest or most innovative—they're the ones that feel impossible to ignore.

THE BUDGET QUESTION IS A MIRROR

The budget conversation doesn't reflect your pricing.

It reflects your *positioning.*

If you hear:

- "We need to wait."
- "We'll revisit this."
- "Let me talk to Finance."

Ask yourself: *Have I made the problem urgent enough? Visible enough? Costly enough?*

Because here's the reality: *If you're not getting budget, it's not a pricing issue—it's a priority issue.* And priority is something you control through narrative, framing, and strategy.

HOW TO POSITION AROUND BUDGET OBJECTIONS

1. Quantify the Cost of Delay (Chapter 3)

The simplest way to justify budget is to show that *waiting* is more expensive than *buying now.*

Example: "Every month you wait is costing you $83,000 in wasted headcount time and missed upsell revenue. That's $249,000 this quarter—and your competitors are closing the gap."

Buyers who don't have budget will go fight for it if the alternative is losing a quarter-million dollars. Your message isn't "Buy our product." It's "This problem is draining you right now. Here's proof."

2. Break the Problem into Strategic Outcomes

Budgets are often siloed. But when you link your solution to strategic initiatives, you can pull from multiple budget sources—or even unlock executive investment.

Example:

You're selling a workflow automation tool. It doesn't just save time. It impacts:

- Customer experience (fewer delays).
- Employee satisfaction (less busywork).
- Security (fewer handoffs, fewer errors).
- Revenue velocity (faster deal cycles).

Now you're not asking for a line-item spend. You're aligning with business transformation.

Strategic alignment opens wallets.

3. Show What Your Customers Cut to Make Room for You

Buyers are more willing to create budget when they see others doing it.

Example messaging:

"Most of our clients fund this by cutting legacy tools, reducing outsourcing costs, or reallocating internal headcount.

"One customer reallocated just 3% of their IT services budget to cover the first year—and doubled their support resolution rate in 90 days."

You're not asking them to spend more. You're asking them to spend smarter.

4. Offer a Fast Path to ROI

Nothing softens a budget discussion like a fast win.

If you can show ROI in 30–60 days, the buyer sees the purchase as a bridge to gain—not a drain on resources.

Example: "We typically deliver measurable impact within 45 days of onboarding—and our clients often break even in under 90."

Now you're not fighting for budget. You're accelerating their return-on-investment cycle. Short time-to-value = less budget resistance.

5. Make Inaction the Riskier Decision

If your marketing has done its job, *doing nothing* should feel like the biggest gamble.

Example:

"You're running a $12M sales operation on systems that haven't been updated since 2018. Every month adds more lag, more friction, and more missed targets.

"What's your team missing while you wait?"

Make waiting feel expensive, reckless, or out of sync with their goals. When the cost of delay is greater than the cost of change, urgency wins.

REAL-WORLD CASE: SECURITY BUDGET REALLOCATION

A cybersecurity platform kept running into "budget freeze" objections. Instead of trying to discount their way in, they asked:

"What's your current annual spend on reactive threat response?"

The buyer said: "Roughly $1.3 million."

The vendor responded:

"We reduce reactive spend by ~30% within 6 months. That's almost $400K. Reallocating 15% of that covers us—and makes your ops team proactive instead of firefighting."

They reframed the conversation from new spend to reallocation from inefficiency. The deal closed—fast.

BUDGET OBJECTIONS ARE A MARKETING OPPORTUNITY

When a buyer says, "We don't have the budget," most sellers hear no.

You should hear:

- "You haven't made this urgent enough yet."
- "You haven't shown me the cost of waiting."
- "You haven't made this feel like a strategic win."

And that's fixable. Marketing isn't just about getting attention. It's about shaping investment. You don't sell to wallets. You sell to priorities.

IF IT'S NOT URGENT, IT'S NOT GETTING FUNDED

In tight markets, only a few things get funded:

- Compliance and Security
- Revenue acceleration
- Cost reduction with provable ROI
- Risk mitigation tied to executive exposure
- Customer retention or experience improvement

So, your job is to tie your solution to one of these. Not in a vague way—but in a *boardroom-ready narrative* that justifies the spend and frames delay as risk.

Action Checklist

- ☐ Show the cost of delay in clear, quantifiable terms.
- ☐ Connect your offer to strategic initiatives, not just a functional team.
- ☐ Help buyers justify the spend with examples of reallocation.
- ☐ Show fast ROI—and how it pays for itself quickly.
- ☐ Reframe "no budget" as "not urgent enough"—and fix that first.

Chapter 11

THE FEAR–CONFIDENCE BALANCE

Fear is one of the most powerful tools in sales and marketing—and also one of the most dangerous. Used well, it creates urgency, movement, and executive focus. Used poorly, it creates paralysis, mistrust, or outright rejection. That's why elite marketers walk a very specific line—one most never even talk about: the Fear–Confidence Balance.

In simple terms:

- Fear gets the buyer's attention.
- Confidence gets them to take action.
- And it's the balance between the two that creates high-velocity decisions.

Push too hard on fear? Buyers freeze or shut down. Push only on confidence? Buyers deprioritize. But when you strike the right balance, buyers move fast—and feel good doing it.

WHY FEAR IS A DOUBLE-EDGED SWORD

Fear-based marketing has been around forever:

- "What if you get hacked?"
- "What if your competitor launches first?"
- "What if you lose that key customer?"

It grabs attention because the brain is wired to detect and prioritize threats. In neuroscience, this is called the negativity bias—the tendency to give more weight to danger than to opportunity.

But fear alone doesn't create decisions. It just creates discomfort. If the buyer doesn't believe they can fix the issue—or doesn't feel safe in choosing your solution—they'll delay, avoid, or shut down. Fear triggers attention. Confidence unlocks movement.

EXAMPLES OF UNBALANCED FEAR

Fear-heavy marketing without confidence sounds like:

- "Your security posture is a disaster."
- "You're three years behind your peers."
- "You're on the verge of noncompliance."

Buyers may nod, but inside they're thinking:

- "I don't know how to fix this."
- "This feels too big."
- "This is going to get me fired if I mess it up."

That's when deals stall. Fear without a clear path forward is paralyzing—not persuasive.

WHAT BUYERS ARE ACTUALLY AFRAID OF

Buyers are rarely afraid of the problem itself.

They're afraid of:

- Picking the wrong solution.
- Wasting budget and political capital.
- Buying something that doesn't get used.
- Looking stupid in front of peers or the board.
- Creating more complexity, not less.
- Becoming dependent on a vendor who disappears.

This is where many marketers get it wrong. They amplify fear—but fail to replace it with confidence. Great marketing does both.

BUILDING THE FEAR–CONFIDENCE ARC

The most effective urgency-driven campaigns follow this pattern:

1. Reveal a problem they didn't realize they had.
2. Frame the consequences of ignoring it.
3. Show how others overcame it.
4. Offer a clear path forward that feels achievable.
5. Provide support and safety along the way.

Let's break each down.

Reveal the Hidden Problem

As discussed in earlier chapters ("The Boiling Frog Effect," "The X-Ray Effect"), urgency starts with surfacing something invisible. Not just telling buyers they have a problem—showing them.

Example: "Your team is spending 11 hours/week manually cleaning CRM data—and 30% of that data still goes unused."

The tone here is factual, not panicked. It's not shame. It's awareness.

Frame the Consequences

Next, you raise the stakes—not with panic, but with clarity.

Example: "That inefficiency is costing you $142,000 per quarter—and eroding rep trust in the system."

Notice: You're still not fearmongering. You're quantifying the impact. You're shifting the conversation from problem to consequence.

Show Social Proof of How Others Prevailed (Confidence Builder #1)

Once buyers feel the discomfort, they need relief.

This is where customer stories, case studies, or peer examples come in.

Example: "One of our customers—same industry, same team size—automated this process in under 30 days. They now run clean data reports with 94% accuracy and cut manual hours in half."

Now the buyer sees two things:

- "I'm not alone."
- "It's possible."

Social proof replaces fear with belief.

Provide a Path Forward (Confidence Builder #2)

Now that belief is rising, it's time to make action feel simple, safe, and supported.

Example:

"Here's how we approach it:

- Week 1: Audit and discovery
- Weeks 2–3: Guided setup with your ops lead
- Week 4: Live data sync, QA, and enablement

"You'll be running clean by day 30—and we'll be by your side the whole time."

Now the solution feels real. Not theoretical. Confidence is rising. Fear is shrinking. Movement becomes inevitable.

Provide Support and Safety (Confidence Builder #3)

Last but critical: You must address the buyer's fear of choosing you.

Do this with:

- Risk-free trials.
- Guaranteed onboarding.
- Clear SLAs.
- Visible roadmap.
- Dedicated support.

Example: "You'll have a dedicated success manager, a 30-day trial period, and a full audit before any commitment. You don't even have to roll it out to everyone. Start with one team."

This calms the brain. It quiets the noise. It creates space for yes.

REAL-WORLD CASE: AIOPS MESSAGING OVERHAUL

An AIOps vendor selling to IT teams realized their messaging was all fear:

- "You're blind to real-time threats."
- "Your alerts are noise."
- "Outages are inevitable."

Their pitch was technically accurate—but emotionally overwhelming.

Buyers froze. So, they rebuilt their narrative:

- *Step 1—Fear (Problem Reveal)*: "Most teams only investigate 3% of alerts. You're working with partial visibility."
- *Step 2—Consequence*: "That means 97% of potential issues go unexamined—until they cause damage."
- *Step 3—Confidence (Social Proof)*: "We helped

[Client X] cut P1 incidents by 62%—with the same team and tools."

- *Step 4—Confidence (Process)*: "Our crawl-walk-run approach means your team never gets overwhelmed."
- *Step 5—Confidence (Reassurance)*: "No system changes. No rip-and-replace. Pilot in one environment. Validate in weeks."

Win rates jumped 37%. Sales cycles shortened by 22%. The difference? Fear + confidence = forward motion.

Buyers don't just need to believe the solution works—they need to believe *they* can champion it successfully. That's the overlooked fear in most enterprise buying decisions: The personal risk. The fear of proposing something new and being wrong. Of spending political capital and not getting results. That's why the strongest marketing doesn't just build confidence in the product—it builds confidence in the buyer. It says: *You've got this. We'll help you prove it. And when it works, you'll look like the visionary who made it happen.*

WHAT CONFIDENCE SOUNDS LIKE IN COPY

- "Most teams feel this. You're not alone."
- "You're closer than you think."
- "Let's simplify this together."
- "You won't go it alone."
- "Here's how we'll make this painless."
- "You'll see results faster than expected."

Reassuring language calms the executive brain. It builds trust. And it turns hesitation into momentum.

WHEN TO DIAL UP FEAR—AND WHEN TO EASE OFF

Scenario	Use More Fear	Use More Confidence
Buyer is unaware of problem	✓	✗
Buyer knows the issue but is scared to act	✗	✓
Buyer is skeptical you can deliver	✗	✓
Buyer is passive or in denial	✓	✗
Buyer is actively researching solutions	Balanced	Balanced

Fear opens the door. Confidence gets them to walk through it. Know which lever to pull—and when.

DON'T SELL SECURITY—SELL PEACE OF MIND

Remember: Don't sell automation. Sell breathing room; don't sell change. Sell confidence that change is possible. Fear wakes buyers up. Confidence moves them forward. Balance both, and you'll create urgency and trust.

Action Checklist

- ☐ Identify the fear your buyer is already feeling but hasn't admitted.
- ☐ Surface it clearly—without panic or shame.
- ☐ Share real-world proof that others have solved it successfully.
- ☐ Give the buyer a path that feels achievable, guided, and low risk.
- ☐ Use reassurance to balance urgency—and drive confident action.

Chapter 12

THE REPRIORITIZATION PLAYBOOK

Your biggest competitor isn't another vendor.

It's not the incumbent. It's not "doing it manually." It's not "we built something internally." Your real competitor—especially in complex B2B sales—is this:

"We have other priorities right now."

That phrase kills more pipeline than pricing objections, feature gaps, or procurement delays combined. It sounds polite. Rational. Strategic. But in reality, it's a stall. And it's your job as a marketer to crack it.

This chapter is about how to move your solution up the priority list—not by begging for attention, but by reframing your narrative so it *earns* it. If you can change how your buyer ranks the importance of solving the problem you address, you'll create urgency where there was once indifference.

WHY BUYERS DEFAULT TO "OTHER PRIORITIES"

Let's start with empathy.

Most decision-makers are juggling the following:

- Dozens of initiatives
- Multiple stakeholders
- Constant inbound from vendors
- Fire drills, meetings, reports, approvals, internal politics

In that chaos, only a few things break through:

- Immediate pain
- Mandates from above
- Opportunities tied directly to KPIs or compensation

Everything else gets pushed. So, when a buyer says, "This isn't a priority right now," they're not lying—they're overwhelmed. They just haven't yet *realized why your solution should be higher on the list.* That's where this playbook comes in.

Step 1: Reframe Your Value in Terms of Strategic Impact

Buyers don't care about your features. They care about their *outcomes.* If your messaging sounds like:

- "We improve process efficiency . . ."
- "We help you scale operations . . ."
- "We optimize communications . . ."

You'll be deprioritized. Why? Because those sound like *nice-to-haves.*

But if you say:

- "We help you retain 15% more revenue by cutting implementation delays . . ."
- "We accelerate Q3 product launches by 3–4 weeks . . ."
- "We cut onboarding drop-off by half in 30 days . . ."

Now you're *speaking their language.*
You've linked your solution to:

- Revenue.
- Launch cycles.
- Retention.
- Metrics that already *are* prioritized.

Don't describe what you do. Describe what you accelerate, protect, or unlock.

Step 2: Tie to an Existing Priority—Not a New One

One mistake sales professionals make is trying to get the buyer to create a new line item on their roadmap. That rarely works. Instead, insert yourself into an existing initiative and show how you *make it work better, faster, or safer.*

Example 1:

Buyer Priority: Digital transformation

Your Reframe:

"This isn't about changing your roadmap. It's about making your digital rollout 40% faster—and getting ROI in 6 months instead of 12."

Example 2:

Buyer Priority: Cost reduction

Your Reframe:

"You're already working on consolidation. We're a proven way to eliminate three tools and reduce software spend by $410K annually."

This changes the conversation from: "This is a distraction" to "This is an accelerator."

Step 3: Use Time-Based Reframing

Often, buyers see your value—but not *urgency*. So you need to compress the timeline.

Instead of saying:

"We help reduce support ticket volume."

Say:

"You're currently getting 2,400 tickets per month. That's 80 per day. Every day you delay is another 6–7 hours of wasted team capacity. In the next 30 days, that's 200+ hours—gone."

Urgency rises when time shrinks. Now you're not solving an annual goal—you're fixing this week's pain.

Step 4: Make Opportunity Cost Tangible

When buyers delay your solution, they don't feel the loss—unless you show it to them.

Example:

"You're saying onboarding improvement is on hold for Q4. Here's what that delay means:

- You'll lose ~12% of applicants in the final stage.
- You'll miss out on ~42 hires in Q3.
- Based on your average revenue per rep, that's $1.2M in delayed production.

"If we start now, we can stop the leakage by next month."

Make the cost of delay greater than the discomfort of reprioritization. That's when decisions get made.

Step 5: Use Executive Alignment Language

Executives don't want to know how your product works. They want to know how it helps them:

- Hit targets.
- Look good.
- Deliver results faster.

- Mitigate risk.
- Reduce exposure.
- Move the business forward.

So, if you want to move up the priority list, use language that resonates at the boardroom level.

Don't say:

"We improve user provisioning."

Say:

"We help you eliminate risk exposure in identity governance—a top audit concern for the board."

Now it's not IT ops. It's executive risk management. Different message. Different priority level.

Step 6: Leverage Peer Stories Strategically

Buyers reprioritize when they feel:

- Competitive pressure.
- Market movement.
- FOMO (fear of missing out).

Use this.

Example: "Three companies in your space have launched AI copilots in the last 60 days. Two of them are our clients. They're seeing engagement metrics double—and marketing is taking credit for the productivity boost."

Now the buyer sees:

- This is already happening.
- Their competitors are ahead.
- Their window is closing.

Fear of irrelevance = reprioritization.

Step 7: Build the "Why Now" Narrative

You can have the best product in the world, but without a "Why Now," you get deprioritized. So, build one. Clearly. Visibly.

Your Why Now might be:

- Market shift.
- Budget cycle.
- Technology sunset.
- Customer expectations changing.
- Growth goal coming faster than they're ready for.
- A campaign or transformation already underway.
- An audit or executive directive on the horizon.

Make it real. Tie your story to it. Create the moment that justifies urgency.

One of the most overlooked levers for reprioritization is the emotional payoff of momentum. When you show buyers how they can make visible progress—fast—you shift them from strategic paralysis to tactical activation. Reprioritization doesn't just come from fear or numbers. It comes from *relief*. If your message helps the buyer feel like they can finally cross a major to-do off their list, show early wins to their boss, or reduce the internal noise they've been quietly tolerating—your solution suddenly becomes not just relevant, but refreshing. And that emotional shift? It's often what gets you to the top of the list.

REAL-WORLD CASE: MARTECH VENDOR REPOSITIONING

A marketing attribution platform was consistently losing deals to "we'll revisit this next year."

They changed their play. Instead of leading with:

"Get visibility into ROI."

They reframed to:

"Every week you don't have visibility, you spend blindly. If you're running 12 campaigns this quarter, and 5 aren't producing—that's 42% of your spend wasted. We'll help you reallocate that budget by next week."

They also tied it to a current initiative:

"This will help your team hit your customer acquisition cost improvement goal for the board—without cutting headcount."

What happened? Meetings increased. Pipeline velocity doubled. Because it was no longer *just another vendor.* It was a *shortcut to a current goal.*

WHEN TO PUSH, AND WHEN TO ALIGN

Situation	Push for Reprioritization	Align with Existing Priority
Buyer is unaware of the problem	✓	✗
Buyer sees value, but no urgency	✓	✓
Buyer has already invested in similar initiatives	✗	✓
Buyer is overwhelmed by too many goals	✓ (if reframed well)	✓
Executive sponsor is involved	✓	✓

The key is flexibility. Sometimes you push. Sometimes you plug in. But either way, your mission is to earn a top 3 slot on their priority list.

Action Checklist

- ☐ Reframe your value in terms of business outcomes, not features.
- ☐ Tie your solution to an existing goal or initiative.
- ☐ Compress the timeline—make results feel near-term.
- ☐ Make the opportunity cost of delay visible and uncomfortable.
- ☐ Use executive language—speak in goals, not features.
- ☐ Share peer success stories to create FOMO.
- ☐ Create a compelling "Why Now" story that forces attention.

Chapter 13

HOW TO WIN THE INTERNAL BUDGET BATTLE

Getting a buyer to want your solution is only half the game. The other half? Helping them win the internal war that actually gets the deal done. Because even after your champion sees the value . . . even after they feel the urgency . . . even after they're nodding on the demo and asking about onboarding . . . they still have to walk into a conference room (or open a Zoom window) and *convince other people to say yes.*

Finance.

Procurement.

Legal.

IT.

The boss.

The board.

You're not just selling to a buyer. You're equipping a buyer to *sell you internally*. And if they lose that battle—so do you.

THE FORGOTTEN BATTLEFIELD OF B2B MARKETING

The internal approval process is where most good deals go to die:

- A skeptical CFO slashes "nonessential" spending.
- A VP in another department blocks it to protect their budget.
- Procurement drags their feet and kills momentum.
- An executive sponsor shifts focus mid-quarter.

These aren't product objections. These are *organizational headwinds.* And yet, most marketers ignore them completely.

They assume:

"If the buyer wants it, the deal will close."

But here's the truth:

The best B2B marketers don't just create demand—they create internal alignment.

They help champions:

- Anticipate resistance.
- Overcome objections.
- Tell a compelling story.
- Rally support.
- Justify budget.
- Neutralize blockers.

They don't just sell to the buyer. They *arm the buyer to win the internal war.*

WHY THIS MATTERS MORE THAN EVER

In today's enterprise sales environment:

- Buying committees average 6–10 people.
- Budgets are tighter and more scrutinized.

- Risk aversion is high, especially in mid-fiscal or pre-close periods.
- Finance teams demand justification and fast ROI.
- Internal politics often trump product fit.

So even when you've "won" the champion, you're often still *miles away from a signed contract.* That's why great marketers plan for the budget battle—not just the buying journey.

IDENTIFY THE BUDGET BATTLEGROUND

Start by mapping out who your champion needs to influence. Usually it includes:

- Their manager or VP.
- The finance approver (CFO, controller).
- A procurement contact.
- Sometimes Legal.
- Often IT or Security (for SaaS or data-related tools).
- Occasionally a cross-functional steering or executive committee.

Each has different concerns. And each can tank your deal. You need to help your champion address *each one's priorities*—not just their own.

GIVE THEM THE "BUDGET JUSTIFICATION TOOLKIT"

Most buyers know your product. What they don't have is the *narrative* to win the room. So, give it to them.

Here's what goes in a good Budget Justification Toolkit:

Business Case Slide or Summary

Clearly show:

- What problem this solves.
- What it costs to delay.
- What ROI is expected.
- When ROI arrives.
- What other vendors were considered (optional).

Make it executive level—no product screenshots, no jargon.

Cost Breakdown and Optional Packages

Have them show:

- Total cost.
- Implementation timeline.
- Optional phased rollouts.
- Clear, transparent pricing (no surprises).

This removes fear and shows flexibility.

Comparison or Replacement Framing

If your solution replaces existing spend, *say so.*

Example: "This replaces Tool X at 80% of the cost, while adding automation and reducing overhead by 42 hours per month."

This allows Finance to view the spend as a reallocation, not a new expense.

Timeline Slide or Visual

Show exactly how the project unfolds:

- Week 1: Audit
- Weeks 2–3: Setup
- Week 4: Live
- Weeks 5+: Value realization

The faster the impact, the easier the approval.

ARM THEM FOR RESISTANCE

Your champion will face objections. Don't let them go in blind.

Common Pushback and How to Overcome It:

Objection 1: "We don't have budget."
Response:
"This initiative pays for itself in under 90 days. Here's how . . ."
"We're reallocating spend from a less effective solution."
"We can start small and scale as impact proves out."

Objection 2: "This isn't a priority."
Response:
"Delaying this will cost us $240K in lost productivity this quarter."
"This ties directly to our Q3 goal of reducing churn."
"Competitors are already doing this—we'll be behind."

Objection 3: "We're already doing something similar." Or "What we have is good enough."
Response:
"Here's how this integrates and adds capabilities—not overlap."
"Current tools don't address X, which is where we're bleeding time."

Your job isn't just to *make the case.* It's to help your buyer *handle the resistance.*

GIVE THEM INTERNAL "SOUND BITES" THAT SELL

Executives won't read a white paper. But they'll repeat a great one-liner in a budget meeting. Give your buyer *internal ammo.*

Examples:

- "Every week we wait, we lose $9,000 in lead response delay."
- "This gives us the data our board keeps asking for—without extra headcount."
- "Our competitors rolled this out last quarter—we're behind."
- "It's not just cost saving. It's about not missing Q2 targets."

When your buyer uses your words to win the room—you win the deal.

MAKE THE INVESTMENT FEEL SAFE

To clear final budget hurdles, you must reduce perceived risk. Ways to do this:

- Pilot or phased rollout
- Opt-out clause after 60 days
- Customer references ready
- Clear SLAs and success criteria
- Dedicated customer success manager
- "Only pay after implementation" clause (if feasible)

Remember: Procurement and Finance don't need to love your product. They just need to *not fear it*. The more risk you remove, the more green lights you get.

Too often, sellers forget this golden rule: Your champion is not a professional buyer—they're an internal persuader. That means they need your help not just to understand your product, but to *defend it* under pressure. Give them tools that win arguments in three minutes or less. Craft talking points they can copy-paste into budget memos. Anticipate the top three blockers and coach your champion on exactly what to say. Your goal is simple: When they step into that internal meeting, they shouldn't feel like they're pitching your product. They should feel like they're pitching their own success—and you're the partner making it possible.

REAL-WORLD EXAMPLE: SAAS PLATFORM ARMS ITS CHAMPIONS

A mid-market SaaS company selling to marketing ops teams kept losing deals in finance review.

So, they built a *Budget Battle Pack*:

- One-slide executive summary
- ROI calculator with editable assumptions
- Three customer quotes in relevant industries
- A 30-60-90-day onboarding plan
- Objection-response doc with suggested responses
- Email templates for requesting executive sign-off

Close rates increased by 29%. Sales cycle time dropped by 21%. The difference? They didn't just pitch. They *equipped their champions to win.*

WHEN TO ACTIVATE THE BUDGET BATTLE PLAN

Stage	Action
Post-demo	Send the Budget Justification Toolkit.
Pre-CFO review	Offer to help roleplay objections.
Procurement loop	Provide one-pager and timeline visual.
Executive sponsor request	Summarize in bullets, not decks.
Cross-functional questions	Offer references and success stories.

You're not just handing off the deal. You're staying in the fight—*through* your buyer.

Action Checklist

- ☐ Map out the buyer's internal approval chain.
- ☐ Build a Budget Justification Toolkit: cost, ROI, timeline, value.
- ☐ Arm your buyer with responses to common objections.
- ☐ Craft internal sound bites that sell in one sentence.
- ☐ Reduce perceived risk with pilot language, references, and SLAs.
- ☐ Offer to assist in prepping for finance or exec meetings.
- ☐ Celebrate when your buyer wins—because that's when you do.

Chapter 14

SIMPLIFYING THE FIRST STEP

You've nailed the pitch. The buyer is interested. The problem is clear. The urgency is there. And then . . . nothing. No signature. No kickoff. No movement.

Why?

Because the *first step feels too big.*

The #1 reason buyers stall—even when they're sold—isn't doubt. It's friction.

They don't know:

- Where to start.
- Who needs to be involved.
- What implementation looks like.
- How risky or disruptive it will be.
- If it's going to derail other work.

And if the first step feels heavy? *They freeze.*

In this chapter, you'll learn how to eliminate that friction and create fast, confident momentum—even in complex B2B environments. Because urgency doesn't just require emotion. It requires *ease of action.*

WHY FIRST-STEP FRICTION KILLS DEALS

Even when a buyer is intellectually sold, their internal narrative sounds like this:

- "I don't have time to figure this out."
- "My team's already stretched."
- "Procurement is going to be a nightmare."
- "We'll need IT—and they're slammed."
- "We should probably wait until next quarter to roll this out."

In other words, the *pain of doing it* outweighs the *pain of the problem.*

Your job isn't just to sell the product. It's to make starting feel so easy, so obvious, and so lightweight that saying "yes" becomes the path of least resistance.

THE THREE TYPES OF FIRST-STEP FRICTION

1. Organizational Friction

This includes:

- Who needs to approve.
- Which team owns the initiative.
- Who will implement it.
- How long it will take.
- What internal resources are needed.

Even if your solution is "self-serve," buyers imagine meetings, alignment, and roadblocks.

2. Technical Friction

This includes:

- Integration complexity.
- Data access issues.
- IT involvement.
- Migration or setup effort.
- Concerns about downtime or system impact.

Technical teams often block progress because they see new tools as risk multipliers.

3. Psychological Friction

This is the invisible drag of:

- Fear of change.
- Fear of failure.
- Not wanting to be blamed if it doesn't work.
- Impostor syndrome ("I don't want to look like I don't understand this tool").

Even the most excited champion can get cold feet if the first step feels like a leap instead of a stride.

THE CURE: REMOVE, REDUCE, OR REDESIGN THE FIRST STEP

The solution isn't to push harder. It's to simplify the start.

Make the first step:

- So easy it feels like no step at all.
- So guided that the buyer never feels alone.
- So contained that it doesn't require political capital.
- So fast that it pays off before people lose interest.

This is where smart marketing, sales enablement, and product strategy intersect.

HOW TO SIMPLIFY THE FIRST STEP IN PRACTICE

Offer a "No Risk" Diagnostic

Give buyers a way to engage without committing.

Examples:

- Free audit or scan
- Risk assessment
- ROI calculator using their data
- Benchmark report based on a 15-minute discovery call

This is value-first marketing. You're not asking them to "start." You're offering to reveal something helpful—no strings.

Example:

"Let's run a 15-minute snapshot on your last 90 days of lead data. We'll show you:

- Your average follow-up delay.
- Opportunities lost due to slow outreach.
- Where deals die—and why.

"No commitment. Just clarity."

Clarity leads to momentum.

Break Implementation into Micro-Stages

Don't pitch the entire rollout. Pitch the *first milestone.*

Example structure:

- Days 1–5: Connect one data source.
- Days 6–10: Run live sample.
- Days 11–14: Share results and adjust.
- Days 15+: Discuss next steps.

This structure reassures buyers:

"I don't have to do everything. I just have to do *this one thing*—and the vendor does the rest."

If the first step feels like the whole journey, you'll lose them. But if it feels like a quick walk to proof, they'll keep going.

Visualize the "Ease of Start" in Your Messaging

Don't just say "It's easy." *Show it.* Give buyers a visual or written path that answers:

- What happens in Week 1?
- What do they need to provide?
- Who needs to be involved?
- How long until the first insight/value?

Example:

- Day 1: Connect Salesforce (takes 10 minutes).
- Day 2: Review your first insights with our team.
- Day 3: Go live with one dashboard.
- Day 7: Share results with your CRO.

The more specific, the less scary.

Create a "Fast Start" Offer

Consider offering:

- A no-cost pilot.
- A 30-day implementation window.
- Done-for-you setup.
- A limited launch in one team or geography.
- White-glove onboarding support.

Framing example:

"We'll set everything up for you. You don't need internal resources. Start with just one use case or team. We'll guide every step—and show impact in under 14 days."

This makes it almost impossible to say no.

Use Customer Quotes That Emphasize Ease

In testimonials, don't just highlight results. Highlight how easy it was to get started.

Examples:

- "I was dreading implementation—but it was done in 3 days."
- "Our team was live in under a week."
- "Honestly, setup took less time than our Monday meetings."
- "The onboarding support was the best we've seen."

Buyers want to hear that *people like them got moving fast*. Because that makes them believe *they can too.*

Buyers don't fear your product. They fear the disruption. Even if they love the idea, they dread adding work, chasing approvals, or becoming the bottleneck. That's why the real unlock isn't proving value—it's proving *ease.* Make them feel like they're gliding into action, not diving into complexity. When the first step looks like progress without pain, the mental resistance vanishes—and forward motion begins.

REAL-WORLD CASE: EMAIL AUTOMATION PLATFORM

An email automation platform struggled with conversions after demos. Buyers were excited—but stalled when it came time to activate.

So, the company introduced a "Fast Start Package":

- Setup by the vendor
- Live in 3 days
- Prebuilt templates

- 30-day pilot, no credit card required
- Results review call after 10 days

Results:

- Demo-to-trial conversion up 55%
- Trial-to-paid conversion up 38%
- Sales cycles 22% shorter

Lesson? The value didn't change. But by *removing all resistance to starting*, they unlocked action.

SHIFT THE BUYER'S QUESTION

Instead of thinking:

"Do we want to do this big thing right now?"

They should be thinking:

"Do we want to take this one small step—and see what happens?"

That's the shift that makes "yes" easy.

When in doubt, ask yourself:

- What's the minimum viable action my buyer can take to get value?
- How can I make that action feel fast, safe, and supported?
- What can I do to show results in under 14 days?
- What part of onboarding can we handle instead of them?
- What support tools, visuals, or messaging can remove friction?

Your first step is everything.

Action Checklist

- ☐ Identify all first-step friction points: organizational, technical, psychological.
- ☐ Replace "Start now" with "Just try this"—use low-risk diagnostics.
- ☐ Build a "Fast Start" version of your solution with clear, small steps.
- ☐ Visualize or document onboarding to make it feel manageable.
- ☐ Include testimonials that emphasize ease of setup and speed of value.
- ☐ Offer white-glove support, pilots, or setup guarantees.
- ☐ Focus messaging on *momentum*, not *magnitude*.

Chapter 15

FROM INACTION TO ESCALATION

Your buyer sees the value. They've agreed the problem is real. They've nodded along in the demo. They've said, "This is great." But . . . nothing happens.

You follow up. They say they're "working on it." They're "aligning stakeholders." They're "circling back after vacation."

The deal stalls. And worse—it stalls quietly. Welcome to the dead zone between interest and action—where deals go to die unless they're escalated.

This chapter is about how to break that inertia, reignite energy, and move deals from polite interest to executive urgency. Because in complex sales, enthusiasm isn't enough. You need escalation.

WHY DEALS STALL AFTER INITIAL EXCITEMENT

Buyers get excited. But that doesn't mean they're ready to act.

What stops them?

1. *Internal Politics*: They don't want to ruffle feathers, cross departments, or trigger new reviews.
2. *Fear of Risk*: They worry about being blamed if it doesn't go well.

3. *Overwhelm*: Too many competing initiatives make yours fade into the background.
4. *Lack of Executive Visibility*: Their boss doesn't care about the problem—or doesn't know it exists.
5. *Default to Comfort*: Change feels like work. And unless something breaks or someone pushes, the status quo wins.

This isn't your fault. But it is your problem. And solving it means engineering escalation.

WHAT ESCALATION MEANS (AND DOESN'T)

Escalation doesn't mean going around your buyer. It means giving them the tools and language to elevate the conversation inside their org. When done right, escalation looks like:

- A director brings the solution to their VP.
- A VP frames it as strategic to the C-suite.
- An exec pushes budget and fast-tracks procurement.

Escalation moves your deal into rooms where urgency lives.

REDEFINE THE PROBLEM AT THE EXECUTIVE LEVEL

If your buyer is stuck, it's often because they're framing the problem too small. Your job is to help them reframe it as a strategic issue, not just a departmental pain.

Don't say: "Your reps are taking too long to follow up."

Say: "You're leaking $220K per quarter in pipeline due to lead lag—and your CMO is presenting that customer acquisition cost number to the board next month."

Now it's not a Sales Ops problem. It's an executive optics problem.

CREATE THE EXECUTIVE TRIGGER

Executives act when one of the following is true:

- A target is at risk.
- A customer is at risk.
- A board goal is slipping.
- A competitor is gaining ground.
- A fire needs to be put out.

So, give your buyer something they can say upstairs that triggers urgency. *Examples:*

- "We're not hitting our onboarding SLAs, and it's putting a renewal at risk."
- "Our peers are already using automation to close twice as fast."
- "Legal is worried about the audit—this closes that gap."

You're not inventing fear. You're giving the buyer a reason to escalate the issue internally.

PROVIDE THE "ESCALATION TOOLKIT"

Your buyer probably doesn't know how to frame this upward. Make it easy. Build a short, clear escalation toolkit they can forward or present.

Your toolkit should include:

- One-slide executive summary.
- Clear risk or opportunity statement.
- Quantified value (money, time, risk reduction).
- Timeline to impact.
- Suggested fast-start approach.
- Minimal resource ask.
- How this aligns to current exec goals.

Keep it tight. Keep it punchy. Keep it boardroom ready.

ADD COMPETITIVE TENSION

Nothing escalates a deal like the fear of being outpaced. If your buyer thinks competitors are ahead, urgency follows.

Use proof points:

- "Three companies in your space have adopted this already."
- "We just rolled this out at [competitor]—they're seeing 22% faster close rates."
- "This will be table stakes within six months. You can lead or chase."

Executives don't want to be embarrassed. They don't want to explain inaction. Use that—responsibly—to move the conversation up the chain.

CREATE A "RISK OF WAITING" NARRATIVE

Escalation gets stronger when the downside of inaction becomes intolerable. Build a short paragraph your buyer can say to their exec:

"If we don't act this quarter, we'll go into Q4 with the same SLA issues. That puts our churn risk at 18%. We've already had two accounts push back on delays. I recommend we fix this now—we have a three-week window to implement with zero disruption."

It's clear. It's tied to risk. It's tied to timing. You just gave them a fast track to escalation.

FUEL ESCALATION WITH CONTRAST AND CLARITY

Escalation also depends on contrast. Show the gap between the current state and the possible future in stark terms—not subtle improvements. Paint two paths:

- Stay here, and incur loss, inefficiency, or risk.
- Move forward, and gain measurable advantage.

Too many sales teams try to persuade through detail. But execs respond to clarity and consequence. Don't give them a 10-slide deck. Give them one slide with three bullets and a decision path. Even better: Give your champion a "board-ready" narrative they can forward or speak to in 30 seconds.

And if there's new data, a new trend, or an urgency signal—put it in front of them. Nothing fuels escalation like a fresh "why now?" moment.

Example: "This quarter's compliance audit was just announced—implementation takes 21 days, and the deadline's 40 days out." Now, it's a real decision.

Escalation works when the stakes are clear, the window is narrow, and the next step is simple.

ESCALATION ISN'T ABOUT DRAMA—IT'S ABOUT VISIBILITY

Most deals don't die because the buyer said no. They die because no one above them ever heard a compelling reason to say yes. If your deal is stuck in polite interest, you haven't escalated the stakes—or the story. Your job is to create the "Oh shit, we need to fix this" moment at the right altitude. That's when things move. Not because someone below pushed harder—but because someone above finally saw it.

REAL-WORLD EXAMPLE: MARKETING OPS DEAL ESCALATION

A marketing automation platform was stuck in director-level reviews. The buyers loved it. But nothing moved. So, they changed their approach:

- Built a one-slide CMO pitch
- Quantified the wasted spend on unused campaigns
- Projected a 19% customer acquisition cost reduction
- Created a 30-day rollout plan with no tech team involvement
- Shared peer results at a competing firm

The director forwarded it. The CMO approved in 48 hours. Procurement fast-tracked it. The team was live in three weeks.

Why? They stopped waiting for the buyer to escalate—and engineered it instead.

COACH THE BUYER ON INTERNAL POLITICS

Your champion may need help navigating:

- Who to include.
- How to present.
- What language to use.
- When to loop in procurement.

Offer help without overstepping:

- "Would it be helpful if I put together a summary for your VP?"
- "Want me to join a short call with Finance to answer questions?"
- "I can prep a quick visual for your CIO if needed."

Most vendors just follow up. Great vendors help their champions win inside their own org.

USE TIME-BASED TRIGGERS TO FORCE MOVEMENT

Create an external reason to move now:

- Discount or fast-start package ends this month.
- Audit or compliance deadline is approaching.
- Q4 budget will close soon.
- Comp plans are changing in 30 days.

If nothing changes, buyers drift. Use time to force escalation.

Example: "If we start this by the 20th, you'll see impact in Q3. After that, we're pushing into end-of-year freeze territory."

Make the cost of waiting feel heavier than the effort of acting.

WHEN YOU STILL HEAR CRICKETS

If you've tried everything and the buyer has gone dark:

- Resurface with new urgency.
- Share something the exec would care about (benchmark, risk, opportunity).
- Offer a way to restart small.

Example: "Totally understand if now's not the time. If it's helpful, I can send a one-page board summary or fast-start offer that you can revisit when budget opens up."

This resets the conversation—without burning the bridge.

Action Checklist

- ☐ Reframe the problem in executive language (risk, revenue, goals).
- ☐ Create a one-slide summary your champion can forward or present.
- ☐ Add competitive pressure or peer examples to trigger fear of falling behind.
- ☐ Craft a "risk of waiting" narrative with clear consequences.
- ☐ Offer to help with internal alignment, prep, or messaging.
- ☐ Tie urgency to a timing trigger (budget close, deadline, initiative).
- ☐ If stuck, provide a graceful off-ramp that leaves the door open for later.

Chapter 16

CREATING EXECUTIVE OWNERSHIP

You don't close big deals by convincing middle managers. You close them when executives take personal ownership of the outcome.

Ownership isn't approval. It's not sign-off. It's not polite interest. It's when a VP or C-suite leader says:

- "We need this."
- "I'm making this happen."
- "Tie this to my KPIs."

At that point, the politics fade. The budget gets cleared. The timeline gets compressed. Because once an executive owns the initiative, it becomes *personal*—and personal priorities rise to the top.

This chapter is about how to create that level of ownership—not by forcing it, but by *earning it through insight, urgency, and alignment.*

WHAT EXECUTIVE OWNERSHIP LOOKS LIKE

Executives have hundreds of initiatives pass their desk. Most are delegated, delayed, or deprioritized. But some—a select few—they grab and say, "I'll take this." You'll know you've crossed into executive ownership when:

- The exec starts asking timeline questions.
- They send the follow-up, not their assistant.
- They bring it up in other meetings.
- They loop in peers or push down directives.
- They tie your solution to a company-wide priority.

This doesn't happen by accident. It happens when your message matches their moment.

THE MISTAKE MOST MARKETERS MAKE

Most messaging is tailored to *users*, not *owners.*

It talks about:

- Features.
- Efficiency.
- Productivity.
- Ease of use.

All important. But executives don't care (yet).

Executives think in terms of:

- Strategic goals.
- Growth levers.
- Organizational risk.
- Competitive position.

- Board visibility.
- Transformation.

If you want them to own the initiative, your story has to speak to *what they're on the hook for.*

TIE YOUR SOLUTION TO EXECUTIVE METRICS

Executives don't care about your product. They care about what their boss expects of them. Your job is to find the *metric, mandate, or priority* they live and die by—and link your solution to it.

Examples:

- "Your CMO wants customer acquisition cost down 22% in 6 months—this gets you halfway there."
- "You're adding 18 new reps next quarter—we can onboard them 4× faster."
- "Your churn goal is under 10%—we reduce support ticket response time by 37%."
- "You promised the board an AI initiative—this is a fast, proven win."

You're not selling software. You're *helping them hit a goal with their name on it.*

DELIVER INSIGHT, NOT JUST INFORMATION

If you want executives to engage, don't educate them. *Teach them something they didn't know.* Bring data, benchmarks, or comparisons they don't have access to.

Examples:

- "You're spending $1.8M annually on manual QA. The top quartile in your industry spends half that—and gets faster releases."
- "Your customer satisfaction dropped 8% in Q2. We correlated that to support delays driven by four key workflows."
- "Your competitors are shifting to event-driven architecture. You're still batch-processing. Here's what that's costing you."

Executives want to work with vendors who make them *smarter, faster.* Bring insight. Spark a realization. Now they're paying attention.

Executives don't just buy solutions—they bet on insight. If you can deliver an "aha!" moment that reshapes how they see their own business, you'll be remembered. You won't just be another vendor—you'll be the one who showed them something others didn't. That's the moment ownership begins. Not when they understand your pitch—but when they see their world differently because of it.

MAKE THE OUTCOME INEVITABLE

Once they're engaged, show them a path that feels achievable and unavoidable. Build a short, visual timeline:

- Phase 1: Audit (1 week)
- Phase 2: Pilot (2–3 weeks)
- Phase 3: Scale (4–6 weeks)
- Phase 4: Measurable impact (from Week 8+)

Make the path look:

- Safe.
- Simple.
- Already in motion elsewhere.

Executive ownership increases when risk feels low, and results feel likely.

GIVE THEM LANGUAGE THEY CAN USE WITH THEIR BOSS

Even execs have to sell up. Give them phrases and proof points they can use in a board meeting, budget review, or steering committee.

Examples:

- "This aligns with our Q3 revenue acceleration initiative."
- "It's self-funding in 60 days based on X savings."
- "This is how [competitor] is moving 2× faster than us."
- "I can deliver this without adding headcount."

The easier it is for an exec to explain why this matters, the more likely they are to take ownership.

USE PEER VALIDATION TO ANCHOR CREDIBILITY

Executives trust peers more than vendors. Use proof points like:

- "The CIO at [industry leader] rolled this out in six weeks and said it's been their most impactful change of the year."
- "A VP of Ops in your space cut three tools and saved $800K—and their COO led the charge."
- "This is now being presented in board decks at three of your closest competitors."

Position your product as a tool for executive success, not just team performance.

SHOW WHAT HAPPENS IF THEY WAIT

Executives aren't scared of making decisions. They're scared of *missing moments*. Make waiting feel like a strategic risk.

Examples:

- "Every quarter you delay, your data gets harder to trust—and harder to use for board-level decisions."
- "If you don't act by October, your Q1 hiring plan gets pushed back 6–8 weeks."
- "You're budgeting now for FY26. This shapes what gets funded—or forgotten."

You're not saying, "Buy now." You're saying, "This is the moment to lead."

REAL-WORLD EXAMPLE: ENTERPRISE SAAS AND THE CRO TRIGGER

A sales acceleration platform landed dozens of mid-level users—but struggled to scale up. So, they built a CRO-specific play:

- Identified top board metrics across accounts
- Created one-page revenue optimization plans
- Built 60-day rollout roadmaps
- Sent peer quotes from other CROs
- Framed the solution as revenue per rep uplift with minimal training

They skipped features. They skipped demos. They said, "This gets you to 130% quota attainment without adding more reps—in 60 days. Here's how your peers are doing it."

CROs took ownership. Revenue followed.

TREAT THE EXECUTIVE AS THE HERO, NOT THE BUYER

Your messaging should cast the exec not as a "customer" but as a leader, a visionary, a force for transformation. Use phrases like:

- "You're leading the charge."
- "This aligns with your legacy initiatives."
- "This is how you future-proof your team."
- "You'll be the first to bring this to your region."

Make them feel like this is their move. Their win. Their play. Ownership rises when ego and impact align.

Action Checklist

- ☐ Identify the top metric or mandate your executive prospect is responsible for.
- ☐ Build a one-pager that ties your product to that outcome.
- ☐ Deliver insight that teaches them something new—not just product info.
- ☐ Visualize a low-risk, high-confidence path to results.
- ☐ Provide internal language they can use to justify the investment.
- ☐ Share peer stories that show similar leaders winning with your solution.
- ☐ Make waiting feel like a missed opportunity.
- ☐ Frame the executive as the driver of the initiative—not the approver.

Chapter 17

THE EMOTIONAL MATH OF URGENCY

People think B2B decisions are rational. That executives evaluate based on logic, ROI, and risk. That if the numbers make sense, the deal moves forward. But that's not how it works. The truth is:

Every buying decision is emotional—and every urgency play has a psychological cost-benefit analysis attached.

You must speak to both the buyer's head and heart:

- "This makes business sense."
- "This feels right—and necessary—now."

This chapter is about decoding the *emotional math* behind urgency. What buyers are weighing. Why they stall. And how to tip the balance in your favor so they act fast, without regret.

WHY RATIONAL MESSAGING ISN'T ENOUGH

You can show:

- ROI projections.
- Competitive comparisons.
- Implementation timelines.
- Benchmarks and data.
- Compliance gaps.

And still . . . the deal doesn't close. Why? Because the *math checks out—but the emotions don't.*

Buyers feel:

- Overwhelmed.
- Unready.
- Nervous.
- Cynical.
- Afraid of disruption.
- Worried they'll be blamed if it goes wrong.

They don't say these things out loud. But it's what slows them down. Every time. If you ignore these emotions, your pitch dies in "We'll circle back later."

That's why urgency must do more than make sense—it must *feel* undeniable. You're not just trying to prove that your solution is smart. You're trying to make the buyer feel like *not acting* is uncomfortable, risky, even irrational. This isn't about hype. It's about emotional alignment. The buyer has to feel the tension of waiting more acutely than the tension of acting.

THE HIDDEN EMOTIONAL EQUATION EVERY BUYER DOES

Inside the mind of every buyer is a silent equation:

Perceived Pain of Problem

+

Perceived Credibility of Solution

+

Perceived Confidence They Can Execute

vs.

Perceived Risk of Change

+

Perceived Disruption to Team

+

Perceived Personal Risk If This Fails

If the top is greater than the bottom, they move the deal. If not, they delay. Your job is to tip the scale—emotionally and logically—so urgency becomes inevitable.

Let's break down each side of the equation.

SIDE 1: MOTIVATORS THAT CREATE URGENCY

Perceived Pain of Problem

Do they feel the problem? Not just understand it—*feel* it. That's where diagnostics, scans, benchmarks, and data exposure come in.

Example: "You're losing $220K/quarter in churn—and your board is asking why."

Perceived Credibility of Solution

Do they believe this will actually fix the issue? That's where proof points, testimonials, references, and visuals matter.

Example: "Here's how [peer company] solved the exact same issue in 30 days."

Perceived Confidence They Can Execute

Do they believe *they* can implement it? That *their* org can adopt it? That's where onboarding simplicity, pilot programs, and "We do the heavy lifting" messaging land.

Example: "We'll set everything up for you. All we need is one hour from your admin team."

SIDE 2: FRICTION THAT DELAYS ACTION

Perceived Risk of Change

Is this going to break something? Disrupt key workflows? Create new vulnerabilities? Minimize these questions with:

- No-risk trials.
- Easy rollbacks.
- Sandboxed pilots.
- IT approvals precleared.

Example: "This won't affect any live systems. Pilot in a sandbox, validate results, then expand."

Perceived Disruption to Team

Will this overload a stretched team? Require change management? Minimize with:

- Small start.
- Team enablement.
- Done-for-you implementation.

Example: "We'll train your team. No change to daily workflows until you're ready."

Perceived Personal Risk If This Fails

This is the killer. What happens to the buyer if they bet on you—and it goes badly? They don't want to look foolish. Lose influence. Hurt their brand. Ease this by showing:

- Others who succeeded.
- Exec-level buy-in.
- Support guarantees.
- Shared accountability.

Example: "We work with your team to define success criteria—and tie 50% of our fee to hitting it."

HOW TO TIP THE EMOTIONAL MATH IN YOUR FAVOR

Now that you know the equation, here's how to move it:

Increase the Felt Pain of the Problem

Don't just say "inefficiency." Say:

"You're losing $19,300 a week in idle technician time—and it's compounding."

The more specific the pain, the more real the urgency.

Boost Confidence in the Outcome

Use before/after snapshots. Use quotes like:

"I thought this would take months. We were up and running in days—and saved six figures in our first quarter."

Specific outcomes drive belief.

Reassure Around Personal Risk

Say:

"We've done this with 47 companies. You'll have a dedicated success manager. And if it doesn't work, you can cancel."

This gives buyers permission to act without fear.

Use the Power of Visualization

Show the buyer what happens after the decision. Not just the value—the *emotional relief.*

"Imagine never having to chase late approvals again."

"No more Monday meetings about SLA misses."

"Your board slides build themselves—with real-time data."

People buy emotions, not features. Give them a feeling to chase.

REAL-WORLD CASE: SECURITY SOFTWARE AND THE CISO'S FEAR

A security software company kept stalling in late-stage deals. Buyers saw the value. But when it came time to pull the trigger, they froze.

Why? Because the *perceived risk of failure* outweighed the *felt pain of the current state.*

So they changed the pitch.

Old: "We'll help you detect threats faster."

New: "You're currently exposed for 9.4 days per incident. That's 226 hours of risk per breach. If the board finds out, it's not the system that gets blamed—it's the CISO."

They followed with:

- Three peer quotes.
- A 14-day pilot.
- A rollback clause.
- A "CISO-safe" onboarding plan.
- A joint accountability framework.

Deals started closing faster. Why? Because they stopped trying to be just logical—and started being emotionally unignorable.

THE ROLE OF URGENCY IN INTERNAL POLITICS

Remember: Your buyer may want to act—but they're also selling you internally. If the *emotional math doesn't add up for the rest of the committee*, you still lose.

So, build materials that help your buyer:

- Reframe the pain in business terms.
- Reassure Finance and procurement.
- Elevate risk in the right way.
- Show why "this won't make us look stupid."

Make them *feel safe bringing you into the room.*

WHEN YOU SEE THE EQUATION ISN'T TIPPING . . .

Ask yourself:

- Have I shown the *cost of doing nothing* clearly enough?
- Have I demonstrated *quick, visible ROI*?
- Have I removed *implementation fear*?
- Have I addressed *personal downside*?
- Have I linked this to *what they care about now*?

If the answer is no, you still have work to do.

Action Checklist

- ☐ Reframe your message from "logical" to "emotional math."
- ☐ Quantify the cost of delay in terms of real dollars, time, or visibility.
- ☐ Add social proof and "people like me" stories to increase credibility.
- ☐ Reduce perceived risk with pilots, guarantees, or success metrics.
- ☐ Show fast ROI to reduce friction from internal stakeholders.
- ☐ Use visualization to sell a better life, not just a better tool.
- ☐ Build messaging that makes it emotionally *safe* to say yes.

Chapter 18

HOW TO TURN A DEMO INTO A DEADLINE

The demo went well. The buyer was engaged. They asked smart questions. They smiled, nodded, maybe even said, "This is exactly what we need."

And then . . .

Nothing.

No contract. No follow-up urgency. Just a slow fade into "Let's regroup later."

Sound familiar?

This chapter is about fixing that. Because too many demos *end conversations*—instead of escalating them. If you want to drive urgency, you can't treat the demo as a milestone. You have to treat it as a *trigger for action*—a moment that demands a next step, a decision, a deadline.

Here's how to make it happen.

WHY MOST DEMOS DON'T CREATE URGENCY

Let's start with the hard truth: Most demos are too passive.

They show features.

They explain workflows.

They prove functionality.

And then . . . they end with a question like:

- "Any thoughts?"
- "What do you think?"
- "Would love your feedback."

All of which place the burden back on the buyer—and lead to indecision.

Buyers don't need a tour. They need a *decision path*. The demo isn't your finish line—it's your ignition point. It should light a fire under the buyer, not give them time to cool off. That means designing the experience around momentum, not just information. Your goal isn't to impress—it's to activate.

YOUR REAL GOAL IN A DEMO

You're not just showcasing the product. You're:

- Making the pain real.
- Making the solution feel easy.
- Making the ROI feel tangible.
- Making the *next step* feel obvious and time sensitive.

In short: *You're selling a moment—not just a product.* A moment that says: "This matters. This works. Let's move."

FIND THE URGENT PAIN AND GET TO THE WOW FAST

One of the biggest reasons demos fail to create urgency?

They're built to show everything—instead of showing what matters right now.

Buyers don't want a tour. They want a mirror. They want to see their urgent pain reflected back in seconds. Not in slide 47. Not after the third feature walk-through.

Start every demo by anchoring on *why this matters today*. Ask questions like:

- "What's keeping your team from hitting your number this quarter?"
- "Where are the biggest breakdowns in your process?"
- "If this works, what changes first—and for whom?"

Your goal is to *find the pain that feels urgent*, then show how your solution solves exactly that—fast.

Don't aim to impress. Aim to trigger a reaction:

"Wait . . . you can do that?"

That's your wow moment. That's the hook.

And the faster you get there, the more likely your buyer is to stop browsing and start buying. If you try to show everything, you dilute the impact. But if you go straight to the pain, and solve it fast, you earn the right to expand.

REDEFINE THE DEMO OUTCOME

The demo isn't the goal. The demo is a *setup*.

So ask yourself: "What do I want them to do *immediately after* this demo?"

- Schedule a trial.
- Loop in Finance.
- Request executive approval.

- Kick off onboarding.
- Approve a scoped pilot.
- Lock in a pricing window.

Once you know your intended outcome, you can guide the conversation toward it—instead of hoping they find their own way.

FRAME THE DEMO AS A DECISION POINT—NOT A TOUR

Before the demo even begins, set the tone.

Example: "The goal of today's session isn't just to show you the platform—it's to help you decide if this solves a real, urgent problem right now. If it does, I'll walk you through next steps we can take immediately after."

This sets expectations:

- This isn't just informative—it's decisive.
- There is a next step—not just follow-up emails.
- The buyer is an active participant—not a passive observer.

Now the demo has direction.

SHOW, THEN QUANTIFY

As you show features, don't just say:

"Here's how it works."

Say:

"Here's what this means for you in real numbers."

Examples:

- "This workflow saves your customer service team 4–6 hours per week per person."

- "That one alert reduction eliminates ~1,000 false positives a month."
- "This report automates what takes your analyst ~8 hours every Friday."

Tie every capability to:

- Time saved.
- Risk reduced.
- Revenue protected.
- Stress eliminated.

The buyer shouldn't just see functionality—they should feel relief.

INTRODUCE A TIME-BASED TRIGGER MID-DEMO

Don't wait until the end. Introduce urgency *as you're showing the solution.* *Examples:*

- "You mentioned your board review is in three weeks. If we move this week, we can be live with reports before then."
- "Budget season's wrapping soon—we can get this into your plan now, or it slips into next year."
- "We're running a pilot program for two other companies in your space. If you want to be included, we'd need to scope this by Friday."

This shifts the buyer from *watching* to *deciding.*

END WITH A CLEAR, TIME-BOUND PATH

At the end of the demo, do not say:

- "Let me know what you think."
- "I'll send you a summary."
- "We'll follow up next week."

Instead, say:
"Here's how teams like yours typically move forward:

- Today: Decide if this solves your top problem.
- Tomorrow: Confirm pilot scope.
- Friday: Approve and kick off.
- Day 14: Live with value metrics reporting.

"Based on your timeline, we'd want to confirm alignment by [date]. Does that work for you?"

Now there's a *clock.* Now there's a structure. Now the buyer has a *decision to make—not a follow-up to dodge.*

FOLLOW UP WITH FRICTIONLESS ACTION

Within two hours of the demo, send:

- A quick summary (bullets only).
- Specific ROI or value reminders.
- A fast-start proposal (pilot, rollout, pricing).
- A scheduling link or contract.
- Optional: "What you'd miss if you delay" message.

Frame your subject line accordingly:

- "Here's your fast path to results—ready when you are."
- "Recap: The $340K problem we can fix this quarter."
- "Pilot window closes Friday—you're in if you want it."

Make it so easy to say yes that the default is movement.

REAL-WORLD EXAMPLE: FINTECH SALES DEMO THAT CLOSED FAST

A fintech vendor was demoing their reconciliation automation platform.

Their old approach:

- Demo features
- Email follow-up
- Wait for "procurement review"

New approach:

- Started demo by saying: "The goal of this demo is to help you decide if this removes 80% of your month-end close pain—so we can act today if it does."
- Showed time savings in real numbers.
- Anchored urgency to board reporting deadlines.
- Presented a pilot offer that expired in 72 hours.
- Used "this is what you'll get in 14 days" roadmap slide.

The buyer escalated to finance that afternoon. The contract was signed within 48 hours. It wasn't the product that changed. It was the urgency play wrapped around the demo.

PREEMPT THE "LET ME THINK ABOUT IT" STALL

If you sense hesitation at the end, say:

"Totally fair to want a moment to process—but I'd love to walk you through what's actually involved in getting started. That way, even if we pause, you're set when you're ready."

Then show:

- How minimal the lift is.
- What support looks like.
- How quickly value arrives.
- How others have succeeded quickly.

This neutralizes fear. And it often turns "I'll think about it" into "Let's do this."

ADD SCARCITY (ONLY IF TRUE)

Scarcity creates motion. But only if it's real.

Use:

- "Only two pilot slots left this quarter."
- "Pricing changes next month."
- "Board deadlines mean we'd need to start by [date]."
- "We only run onboarding once a month for this cohort."

Don't fake it. But don't hide it either. If there's real pressure, share it. Buyers don't like to miss windows.

Action Checklist

- ☐ Define the *real goal* of the demo—what happens right after.
- ☐ Set expectations up front: This is about decision, not just education.
- ☐ Quantify value in time, dollars, or risk with every feature you show.
- ☐ Introduce a time-based reason to act before the demo ends.
- ☐ Close with a decision path, not a vague follow-up.
- ☐ Follow up with a clear plan, frictionless next step, and deadline.
- ☐ If needed, offer safe pilots, fast wins, or small starts.
- ☐ Use real scarcity—only if it's authentic.

Chapter 19

TURNING BUDGET OBJECTIONS INTO MOMENTUM

"We don't have budget for this right now."

"Let's revisit this next fiscal year."

"It's not in the plan."

Sound familiar? Budget objections are the most common—and misunderstood—barriers in complex sales. But here's the secret:

The problem isn't usually the budget. It's the priority.

Companies find budget when the need is urgent enough. When the ROI is clear enough. When the executive sponsor believes *waiting is riskier than acting.*

This chapter is about how to flip the budget objection: not by discounting, begging, or waiting, but by reframing the conversation to drive momentum, not retreat.

WHY BUDGET OBJECTIONS APPEAR (EVEN WHEN THERE'S MONEY)

Buyers say "we have no budget" when they're really saying:

- "I don't have the internal willpower to fight for this."
- "This hasn't made it to the top of my priorities."
- "I'm not emotionally sold enough to take the next step."
- "I need to defer risk."

This is where most marketers and sellers get it wrong. They hear "no budget" and stop pushing. But a better question is: Why haven't we made this urgent enough to justify budget reallocation? Budget objections aren't stop signs—they're invitations to deepen the business case. When a buyer says, "It's not in the budget," what they're really saying is, "You haven't shown me why this matters more than everything else we're already spending on." That's not a hard no. It's a challenge to be more relevant, more specific, and more tied to what the business already values.

Because budget can always be reshuffled—especially in software and services. Here are six steps for countering budget objections.

Step 1: Reframe "Budget" as "Strategic Relevance"

The fastest way to overcome a budget objection is to reconnect your offer to something that's already funded. Tie your message to:

- Revenue acceleration.
- Risk mitigation.
- Regulatory compliance.
- Cost-cutting initiatives.
- Customer experience.
- Digital transformation.
- AI or automation mandates.

Examples:

- "This isn't new spend—this accelerates your digital transformation plan for Q3."
- "We've helped clients fund this by reducing three other tools—this consolidates their stack."
- "This is how [competitor] justified the investment—they pulled from their ops efficiency budget."

Now the conversation isn't about new dollars—it's about smarter allocation.

Step 2: Quantify the Cost of Delay

The best way to overcome a budget freeze is to make waiting more expensive than acting.

Examples:

- "Every month you delay this, you burn $42K in churned leads."
- "Each quarter without automation is 96 hours in wasted technician time."
- "You'll lose $270K in overages if you wait until Q4 to deploy this."

Create a simple chart:

Wait Time	Estimated Loss
1 month	$43,000
3 months	$129,000
6 months	$258,000

Send this in your follow-up. Let the math do the talking. Now the question isn't, "Can we afford it?" It's, "Can we afford to keep bleeding cash?"

Step 3: Break the Spend into Smaller, Safer Units

Buyers freeze when the investment feels big. Make it feel small by:

- Offering phased rollouts.
- Framing the spend monthly or quarterly.

- Starting with a small use case.
- Offering pilot pricing tied to results.

Example: "Instead of a $48K annual deal, let's start with a 60-day pilot at $4K. If we don't show measurable value, we pause."

You're not selling the whole mountain. You're selling the first step. And the smaller that step feels, the easier it is to budget for—formally or not.

Step 4: Show How Others Unlocked Budget

Use proof points from real customers:

- "CISO reallocated risk audit funds for this rollout."
- "A VP of RevOps pulled from a training budget to cover it."
- "An IT team covered it using savings from cutting two legacy vendors."
- "They got budget by tying this to a broader AI transformation initiative."

This does two things:

1. Makes the budget feel gettable.
2. Makes your buyer feel safe copying others.

Executives don't want to be first. They want to be smart—and not left behind.

Step 5: Offer a "Budget-Ready" Approval Package

Many buyers want to buy—but don't know how to fight the budget battle. So, equip them.

Build a Budget Justification Toolkit (see chapter 13) that includes:

- One-page ROI snapshot.
- Timeline to first value.
- Customer reference quotes.
- Internal email template.

- Comparison to current spend.
- Optional: Net-new vs. reallocation framing.

You're not just giving them data—you're giving them internal ammunition. Now they're not asking for money. They're justifying investment.

Step 6: Use Timing Windows to Create Pressure

Budget stalls feel safe—unless there's a clock. Use real triggers:

- "If we scope this by the 15th, it fits into this quarter's budget."
- "Our pilot window closes next week—that includes onboarding."
- "Your planning cycle starts next month. Let's anchor this in before that."
- "You said the new VP starts in June. If we wait, this resets entirely."

Without a deadline, budget objections are just polite stall tactics. With a deadline, they force clarity.

REAL-WORLD EXAMPLE: HR TECH DEAL THAT REVERSED THE OBJECTION

An HR software platform got a "We don't have budget" from a fast-growing Series C company. Instead of backing off, they responded with:

- A one-slide ROI calculator based on hiring metrics.
- A phased implementation that started at $6K for 30 days.
- Proof of peer companies doing the same.
- A Slack message template for the champion to send their VP.
- A "we can start Monday or wait 90 days" timing offer.

The deal closed in six days. Why? Because they turned "no budget" into "We're losing $14K/month by not fixing this—let's just do it."

WHAT NOT TO DO

Here's what kills urgency when you hear a budget objection:

- Offering a discount without changing the narrative.
- Saying, "Okay, we'll check back next quarter."
- Asking, "When do you think you'll have budget?"
- Assuming procurement = dead end.
- Sounding desperate.

Instead, maintain posture: "Totally understand—most of our clients said the same at first. Let me show you how they justified it, and you can decide if it's worth elevating." Confidence + insight = momentum.

Action Checklist

- ☐ Reframe the investment as strategic—not incremental.
- ☐ Connect the solution to already-funded initiatives.
- ☐ Quantify the cost of delay in real dollars and metrics.
- ☐ Break the offer into smaller, safer spend phases.
- ☐ Use real customer stories to show budget reallocation examples.
- ☐ Build a Budget Justification Toolkit for champions.
- ☐ Add urgency with time-based triggers or windows.
- ☐ Maintain confidence—and reframe the objection as a solvable puzzle.

Chapter 20

WHY YOUR CHAMPION ISN'T ENOUGH

They love the product. They tell you, "This is exactly what we need." They bring good energy on the demo. They promise to share with their team. They say they'll "drive this internally."

And then . . . crickets.

Welcome to one of the most frustrating (but common) stalls in B2B sales: the enthusiastic champion who can't or won't get the deal done. This chapter is about understanding why that happens, how to avoid it, and how to *build a multi-threaded urgency strategy* that doesn't die with one person's delay or hesitation.

Because one champion isn't enough. Not anymore.

WHY CHAMPIONS FAIL TO CLOSE THE DEAL

It's not always their fault. Champions fail for many reasons.

They Don't Have Authority

Many buyers *can't say yes*—they can only recommend.

They may be a director, a manager, or an end user. They love the solution, but they don't control:

- Budget.
- Final decision.
- Cross-functional approval.
- IT sign-off.

You've got interest. But not *influence.*

They Can't Build the Business Case

They know the product is good. But they don't know how to:

- Quantify ROI.
- Reframe risk.
- Pitch procurement.
- Answer Finance's questions.
- Align with company goals.

So even if they try to escalate, the deal gets stuck in translation.

They Get Distracted

Most champions are busy. Unless your initiative ties directly to their personal goals, KPIs, or compensation, it gets deprioritized. They mean well—but they don't follow through. Not because of disinterest, but because of *urgency drift.*

They Don't Want to Stick Their Neck Out

They fear being wrong. They fear buying something that doesn't deliver. They fear pushing too hard and losing internal credibility. So, they stay quiet. Or soft-pitch it. Or delay. And the deal dies—not from rejection, but from timid internal sponsorship.

THE FALSE SENSE OF SECURITY A CHAMPION CREATES

Champions can lull you into comfort. They say:

- "We're excited."
- "This is moving."
- "I'm sharing it this week."
- "I've got a meeting with my VP."

You stop pushing. You wait. But here's the reality: A champion without access, courage, and support is not a deal driver. You don't need cheerleaders. You need mobilizers. And that requires a different approach. Your job isn't just to win the room—it's to win the org. A single champion might get you a meeting, but they rarely get you a contract. That's why high-performing teams don't just ask, "Do they like us?"—they ask, "Who else needs to believe this matters now?" If your champion can't answer that, you don't have alignment—you have an illusion.

Here are five steps to creating a strong internal champion and consensus from key deal influencers.

Step 1: Profile Your Champion Early

Ask yourself:

Question	Champion Score
Can they approve budget?	✓ / ✗
Do they have VP+ influence?	✓ / ✗
Do they tie your solution to strategic goals?	✓ / ✗
Can they quantify value or own the business case?	✓ / ✗
Do they bring in cross-functional stakeholders?	✓ / ✗
Are they proactively pushing?	✓ / ✗

If you answered most questions with an ✗, you don't have a true champion. You have a fan. Fans are great. But they won't get your deal done.

Step 2: Help Champions Elevate—or Expand Beyond Them

If your champion is stuck, *don't replace them—empower them.* Ways to help:

- Provide a business case deck.
- Write internal emails for them to send.
- Offer to join their internal pitch calls.
- Create a one-pager for their executive.
- Give them proof points they can use.

If they still don't move? Expand the thread. Tactfully ask:

- "Who else should be in this conversation to align with your leadership's goals?"
- "Would it help to bring in [IT/Finance/Compliance] now, so we're not delayed later?"
- "Are there any sponsors who've pushed similar initiatives that we should loop in?"

You're not going around them. You're helping them build consensus.

Step 3: Create Internal Urgency Beyond the Champion

The best way to de-risk single-threaded deals is to trigger urgency at the organizational level. Do this by:

- Sharing competitive pressure ("Your peers are doing this—here's what they're seeing.").
- Linking your solution to company-wide KPIs.
- Showing exec-level risk if the problem isn't solved.
- Offering to run executive briefings or ROI workshops.
- Tying into planning, transformation, or compliance windows.

You're elevating the narrative, so more people care—and more people push.

Step 4: Use Multi-threading as Your Default Strategy

In enterprise deals, *you never bet on one person.* Even if they're brilliant. Even if they love you. Even if they have budget. You build a coalition of the following people:

- User champion
- Economic buyer
- Executive sponsor
- Cross-functional partner (IT, HR, Legal, etc.)
- Procurement pro

Your job is to *orchestrate urgency across roles.* Because if one person slows down—others keep the momentum.

REAL-WORLD EXAMPLE: SAAS DEAL STALLED BY SINGLE CHAMPION

A SaaS productivity platform had a strong champion in a RevOps director. She loved the product. Demos went great. She promised to bring in her CRO. But she didn't. The vendor waited three weeks. Silence. Then she messaged:

"We've had a reorg. I'll follow up when things settle."

Translation: Dead.

The sales team changed course. They:

- Identified a new buyer in enablement.
- Shared a new ROI calculator tied to onboarding metrics.
- Reached out to the CRO's chief of staff with insight.
- Got reengaged with IT to scope integration.

> The deal revived—and closed in four weeks. Why? Because they stopped relying on one person—and *built a movement.*

Step 5: Use the "Power Triangle" in Messaging

When you engage more stakeholders, match your message to what they care about.

Persona	What They Want
User Champion	Simplicity, daily value, time saved
Executive	Strategic ROI, speed to result, visibility
IT	Low risk, secure, easy integration
Finance	Budget clarity, short time-to-value

Build a deck or message stream that hits all three wants of the stakeholder—the Power Triangle. Now the champion isn't alone. They're part of a team pushing in the same direction.

POLITELY TEST THE CHAMPION'S STRENGTH

If you're unsure whether your champion can close, try this.

Ask them:

- "If your VP says yes, what happens next?"
- "Have you gotten sign-off on similar-sized investments before?"
- "Would you be open to copresenting to the team next week?"

If they avoid, defer, or stall—that's your signal. You're single-threaded. Time to widen the circle.

Action Checklist

- ☐ Score your champion on authority, influence, alignment, and proactivity.
- ☐ Help your champion pitch upward with tools and templates.
- ☐ Ask early who else should be involved—and offer to help.
- ☐ Tie your message to company-wide goals and planning cycles.
- ☐ Create a multi-threaded stakeholder map with tailored messaging.
- ☐ Use executive insights, peer pressure, or compliance triggers to elevate.
- ☐ Run parallel conversations with IT, Finance, or other blockers.
- ☐ Never let one person—no matter how enthusiastic—own your outcome alone.

Chapter 21

THE POWER OF A SHARED ENEMY

Want to create instant clarity, momentum, and urgency? Give your buyers a *villain.* Because nothing galvanizes action faster than a shared enemy—something that threatens your buyer's success, credibility, budget, or future. It can be:

- A competitor eating their market share.
- A broken system holding them back.
- A new regulation they're not ready for.
- A risk they've ignored too long.
- A transformation wave they're behind on.

When you frame the conversation around what they're up against, you move the conversation as follows:

- "This could be helpful" → "This is necessary"
- "Maybe later" → "We have to move now"
- "Another vendor" → "A partner in our fight"

This chapter is about how to find your buyer's enemy—and how to make your solution the weapon that helps them win.

WHY A SHARED ENEMY CREATES URGENCY

Humans are wired for contrast:

- Safe vs. dangerous
- Progress vs. decline
- Us vs. them

When you introduce an adversary, it does three things:

1. *Sharpens focus*: Buyers stop evaluating and start fighting.
2. *Builds unity*: Internal teams rally together around solving the problem.
3. *Increases speed*: Decision cycles shrink because the threat feels imminent.

In complex B2B, where inertia is your biggest foe, a well-defined enemy becomes a catalyst for clarity.

IDENTIFY THE RIGHT KIND OF ENEMY

You're not inventing a bogeyman. You're surfacing a threat your buyers already feel—but maybe haven't named.

The best shared enemies fall into five categories.

1. The External Competitor

- "Your competitors are building AI copilots. You're still running manual reports."

- "They're onboarding reps in three days. You're still at three weeks."
- "They've consolidated tech. You're overpaying and underperforming."

This isn't about FUD (fear, uncertainty, doubt). It's about fueling ambition. Your message becomes, "They're gaining ground—and here's how you catch up or pull ahead."

2. The Internal Obstacle

- "You're stuck in outdated workflows that slow your best people down."
- "Your current process creates nine handoffs before a customer gets value."
- "You've accepted broken as normal—and it's costing you every day."

This enemy is a silent killer. You're not blaming them—you're exposing the invisible thief.

The message becomes, "You've outgrown this. It's time to evolve."

3. The Market Shift

- "Your buyers expect real-time. You're delivering after-the-fact."
- "AI is rewriting the way your industry operates."
- "Compliance is getting tighter, and penalties are increasing."
- "Your customers won't tolerate delays, silos, or generic experiences anymore."

This works because the enemy isn't you—or them. It's change itself. Your message becomes, "You can't stop the shift—but you can choose how fast you adapt."

4. The Missed Opportunity

- "You're sitting on a gold mine of data that no one's using."
- "You're overpaying for tools that don't deliver ROI."

- "You're spending more time managing processes than serving customers."

This isn't a fear play—it's about loss of potential. Your message becomes, "While others optimize, you're leaving money on the table. Let's change that."

5. The Internal Politics or Perception Risk

- "Your CFO sees spend but not results."
- "The board is asking hard questions about risk exposure."
- "Your brand doesn't reflect your innovation story."

Now the enemy is perception. And you're offering clarity, alignment, and credibility.

MAKE THE ENEMY VISIBLE

The enemy only creates urgency if the buyer sees it clearly. That means using:

- Benchmarks.
- Visuals.
- Stories.
- Case studies.
- Data snapshots.
- Buyer quotes from similar roles.

Examples:

- "The average company in your sector cut tool sprawl by 26% last year—but you've added four more tools."
- "Here's what your current onboarding timeline looks like compared to competitors—and what it's costing in quota delay."
- "This is your customer feedback—62% said they're frustrated by response times."

Visibility creates discomfort. Discomfort drives action.

INTRODUCE YOURSELF AS THE WEAPON

Once the enemy is clear, you become the solution. Not just a product—a partner in the fight. Reframe your narrative:

- "We help leaders eliminate legacy tech that holds teams back."
- "We give you the automation layer to outpace competitors."
- "We get you audit-ready in 14 days."
- "We reduce your reliance on overloaded IT and give you freedom to move faster."

You're not just solving a problem. You're arming them for battle.

RALLY THEIR TEAM INTERNALLY

Shared enemies don't just galvanize buyers—they galvanize entire teams. Help your champion bring others into the fight:

- "Let's show your CFO what this inefficiency is costing."
- "Your COO should see this—it ties directly to Q3 productivity goals."
- "Your security team's on the hook for this audit gap."

Now it's not a product decision. It's an organizational movement.

USE LANGUAGE THAT SPARKS EMOTION

Here's the subtle art: The enemy you introduce must feel beatable, not overwhelming.

Bad example: "If you don't solve this, your business is doomed."

Good example: "You're losing ground—but with the right approach, you can leap ahead."

Use phrases like:

- "Gain ground"
- "Take control"
- "Future-proof"
- "Outmaneuver"
- "Cut through the noise"
- "Reclaim your advantage"

Fear opens the door. Belief in a better future keeps it open. Don't just diagnose the enemy—dramatize it. The best marketers don't merely point to a threat; they paint a picture of what life looks like if it goes unaddressed. They make the stakes vivid, the consequences visible, and the cost of inaction personal. Because when the enemy feels close—not abstract—urgency skyrockets.

REAL-WORLD EXAMPLE: DATAOPS COMPANY AND THE ENEMY WITHIN

A DataOps startup was struggling to close enterprise deals. Their product was strong—but the urgency wasn't there. So they changed the story. Instead of pitching features, they painted a villain:

- "Your analysts spend 80% of their time cleaning data—not analyzing it."
- "Meanwhile, competitors are automating that layer and making decisions in hours, not days."
- "This isn't about better dashboards—it's about the internal processes that are bleeding your advantage."

They positioned themselves as "the automation engine that eliminates the bottlenecks your competitors already fixed."

Deals started moving—because now it wasn't about

nice-to-have analytics. It was about winning a battle that was already happening.

DON'T JUST NAME THE ENEMY—KEEP THEM IN THE STORY

Don't make the villain a one-slide gimmick. Weave it through the buyer journey:

- *Discovery call*: Surface the threat.
- *Demo*: Show how it's impacting their world.
- *Proposal*: Quantify what defeating it will yield.
- *Onboarding*: Frame milestones as battle wins.
- *Expansion*: Show how to scale the victory.

People don't just want software. They want to win. You're giving them the story that makes that possible.

Action Checklist

- ☐ Identify your buyer's most pressing enemy: external, internal, market, opportunity, or political.
- ☐ Use data, visuals, and benchmarks to make the enemy real.
- ☐ Position your solution as the weapon—not just the fix.
- ☐ Equip your champion to rally others around the cause.
- ☐ Use emotional, confident language that makes winning feel achievable.
- ☐ Weave the enemy through every stage of your marketing, sales, and onboarding process.
- ☐ Make it clear: Inaction means the enemy wins—and action puts your buyer in control.

Chapter 22

DESIGNING FOR THE SKEPTIC IN THE ROOM

In every B2B deal, there's someone who sits back, arms crossed, barely speaking. They're not sold. They're not impressed. They're not convinced. They're the skeptic in the room. And if you ignore them—or worse, try to steamroll them—they'll kill your deal before it even has a chance. But if you design your pitch, content, and proof around winning them over, something powerful happens:

- You reduce internal friction.
- You strengthen your credibility.
- You force rigor into your value proposition.
- And in many cases . . . the skeptic becomes your strongest advocate.

This chapter is about how to build urgency and buy-in with the hardest-to-convince stakeholders—and turn them from blockers into backers.

WHY SKEPTICS MATTER MORE THAN YOU THINK

Skeptics often aren't loud. They're not leading the charge. But they're influential in ways you can't always see. They might be:

- A quietly powerful engineer.
- A finance controller with veto power.
- An operations lead who resists change.
- A compliance officer focused on risk.
- A VP who's been burned by vendors before.

These people don't want hype. They want proof. Simplicity. Logic. Control. And if you can give them that, they become your unexpected ally.

WHAT SKEPTICS ARE REALLY AFRAID OF

Most skeptics aren't just being difficult. They're protecting something. They're trying to avoid:

- Making a bad decision.
- Creating rework for their team.
- Getting blamed if the tool fails.
- Buying into vaporware.
- Disrupting stable systems.
- Repeating past mistakes.

Understanding their fear is the key to building your strategy. Once you do that, you can preempt resistance—and earn trust. Below are seven steps to help you do so.

Step 1: Acknowledge Their Concerns—Before They Say a Word

The first way to win a skeptic is to *voice their doubts before they do.*

Examples:

- "You might be wondering if this will create extra work for your team . . ."
- "You're probably skeptical—most automation promises are overhyped. Here's how we're different."
- "You've seen vendors make big claims and fall short. Let me show you the data."

This does two things:

1. It shows respect.
2. It removes their need to "be the tough one"—because you already are.

They lean in, not because they agree—but because they realize you're not naive.

Step 2: Show the Math, Not the Marketing

Skeptics don't want slogans. They want specifics. Instead of:

"We save you time."

Say:

"This eliminates 6 manual tasks per workflow, saving 14 hours/month per manager. That's 168 hours/year across your team."

Instead of:

"We help you close deals faster."

Say:

"Companies that implemented this closed 28% more deals within the quarter—with 12% higher revenue."

Bring the following:

- Data
- Benchmarks
- Before/after snapshots
- Cost breakdowns
- Time-to-value tables

Your goal isn't to overwhelm—it's to leave no room for doubt.

Step 3: Share Stories of Other Skeptics Who Converted

The skeptic doesn't care that your customer loves you. They care that someone *like them* started skeptical . . . and became a believer.

Use quotes like:

- "I didn't think this would work. But we were live in nine days—and our error rate dropped by 52%."
- "We'd been burned before. But this team delivered fast, clear ROI—and backed it up with real support."
- "I told my boss I wouldn't roll it out unless I saw value in 30 days. I saw it in 10."

This is powerful because it's identity driven. The skeptic sees someone like them—with the same doubts—who got the win. Now they're listening.

Step 4: Invite Their Scrutiny—and Respect It

Don't try to dodge the skeptic. Bring them in.

Say:

- "I'd actually love your pushback here—you'll probably see things we missed."
- "What's the part that feels least believable or most risky to you?"
- "Can I walk you through how our most skeptical customers validated this before buying?"

This shows strength. You're not afraid of critique. You're *inviting* it—because you're confident in your case. And it makes them feel seen. Respected. Heard. That builds trust—and opens doors.

Step 5: Give Them Something They Can Test—Fast

Skeptics want to try it for themselves. So, make it easy to validate without commitment. Offer:

- A sandbox.
- A limited pilot.
- A proof of concept.
- A diagnostic or benchmark.
- Read-only access to a test dashboard.

Say:

"Don't take our word for it. Let's run your data through the system. If it doesn't deliver insight within 48 hours, we'll stop there."

This lowers the temperature. It makes the first step feel scientific—not emotional. And skeptics love science.

Step 6: Show You're Already Battle-Tested

Another way to earn trust? Show that other demanding, regulated, high-stakes teams already use you.

Examples:

- "We power 5 of the top 10 healthcare systems in the country."
- "We meet GDPR and HIPAA compliance—out of the box."
- "The last three audits our customers faced? Zero issues tied to us."

Now the skeptic thinks: "If it worked for them—under pressure—maybe it's legit."

REAL-WORLD EXAMPLE: DEVOPS SKEPTIC BECOMES SUPERUSER

A DevOps tool was being pitched to a large enterprise. The CTO loved it. The procurement team liked the pricing. But a mid-level engineering lead—silent in the first call—was the blocker. He'd seen bad rollouts before. He didn't trust the vendor. He didn't want his team disrupted. The vendor stopped pushing. And instead, he did the following:

- Built a sandbox using the team's existing stack.
- Offered read-only access for validation.
- Sent anonymized metrics from similar companies.
- Gave him a direct Slack line to the head of product.
- Said: "Prove us wrong. We'll wait."

He tested it. Then championed it. Deal closed. Fast. Skeptic to superuser—because they let him drive the proof.

Step 7: Build "Skeptic-Ready" Messaging into Everything

This isn't just about sales calls. Your entire go-to-market strategy should be skeptic-proof. In your site copy, collateral, emails, decks, ask:

- What's the claim here?
- What would the skeptic say in response?
- How do I answer it clearly, concisely, and with evidence?

Use:

- FAQ-style rebuttals.
- ROI calculators.
- TCO (total cost of ownership) comparisons.
- Security and compliance deep dives.
- "What went wrong and how we fixed it" case studies.

You're not just marketing to champions. You're building a case that holds up to interrogation. That's how you win real consensus. Winning the skeptic isn't just about de-risking. It's about making them feel respected, equipped, and in control. When skeptics shift from feeling like they're being "sold to"—to realizing they're being "counted on"—everything changes. Your job isn't to silence them. It's to empower them. Because once they believe in you, they'll convince everyone else.

Action Checklist

- ☐ Anticipate your skeptic's unspoken fears—and say them out loud.
- ☐ Replace vague claims with data, math, and concrete outcomes.
- ☐ Use stories of former skeptics who became advocates.
- ☐ Invite skepticism with confidence, not defensiveness.
- ☐ Provide low-risk ways to test, validate, or sandbox your solution.
- ☐ Showcase logos, certifications, and success in high-stakes environments.
- ☐ Build skeptic-proof messaging into your marketing assets, FAQs, and proposals.

Chapter 23

ENGINEERING A FIRST WIN FAST

You've got the deal. The contract is signed. Everyone's excited. But now comes the most dangerous phase of all: *the post-sale stall.*

This is where energy fades. Timelines slip. Internal teams lose interest. The buyer starts wondering: Did we make the right call?

And worst of all? Without a *clear*, *fast win*, the urgency you worked so hard to build—dies. That's why the best go-to-market teams don't just close deals—they *engineer a first win.* One that's fast, visible, measurable, and strategic. A first win that creates:

- Internal credibility.
- Buyer confidence.
- Stakeholder alignment.
- Expansion opportunities.
- Ongoing urgency.

Let's break down how to make that win happen—every single time.

WHY FIRST WINS MATTER MORE THAN PRODUCT FEATURES

Early adoption is fragile. Even when the buyer wants to succeed, internal forces conspire against action:

- Competing projects
- Change resistance
- Confusing onboarding
- Poor handoffs from Sales
- Lack of executive oversight
- Fear of disrupting existing systems

And if value doesn't show up quickly, the tool gets labeled as:

- "Too complicated."
- "Not ready."
- "Not a priority."

Which means churn risk rises—before the first renewal even hits the calendar.

But a quick, strategic victory shifts everything:

"This works."

"We picked the right vendor."

"Let's do more."

Here are the steps for engineering the first win.

Step 1: Define the Win Before You Close

Here's the first mistake teams make: They wait until after the deal to define success. That's too late. Instead, during the sales process—especially during the proposal and late-stage calls—ask: "If we had this live in 30 days, what's the *one result* that would make you say, 'This was worth it'?" Let them define it. Then write it down.

That becomes your *North Star* for onboarding. Now it's not a vague promise of "value." It's a concrete goal—with alignment from day one.

Step 2: Keep the Scope Small, the Win Big

A great first win:

- Doesn't involve the whole org.
- Doesn't require tons of integration.
- Doesn't need long change management cycles.
- But still proves a core piece of value.

Examples:

- Launch one automation in a small team.
- Run a diagnostic that reveals hidden cost.
- Replace one legacy workflow.
- Generate one report that saves exec time.
- Fix one compliance gap with measurable impact.

Think precision, not perfection. You're showing what's possible—not solving everything at once.

Step 3: Visualize the First 30 Days

Buyers freeze when they don't know what happens next. So eliminate ambiguity. Send a timeline that looks like this:

Day	Action
1	Kick off & align success metric.
3	Connect systems/set up environment.
7	Run pilot scenario.
10	Review early insights.
15	Optimize and go live.
21	Measure results.
30	Present win to stakeholders.

This creates trust. Clarity. Progress. The buyer feels momentum—and starts believing in the full rollout.

Step 4: Assign Ownership on Both Sides

Deals stall post-close when no one owns the outcome. Fix that.

- Assign a customer success lead (CSM).
- Confirm the buyer's internal champion (and make it their KPI).
- Loop in executive sponsors.
- Hold a joint planning session.

Use a simple agreement:

"Our job is to get you [win] in [time frame]. Here's what we'll do—and here's what we need from your team." Now it's not a handoff. It's a shared mission.

Step 5: Make the Win Visible Internally

A win that no one sees . . . isn't a win. Help your champion:

- Summarize results in a one-pager.
- Present the win to their VP or cross-functional team.
- Highlight metrics in Slack/Teams updates.
- Quote early users or impacted stakeholders.
- Build a "before/after" slide.

Your messaging: "Here's what we fixed. Here's how fast. Here's what we're doing next." Wins create momentum, belief, and political capital. And that's what fuels expansion.

Step 6: Celebrate Progress Loudly and Early

Most onboarding processes are boring, dry, and internal. Flip the script. When the first milestone is hit:

- Send a thank-you video.
- Share a LinkedIn shoutout (with permission).
- Offer a mini case study template.
- Invite them to a customer advisory board.
- Give their team recognition.

Remember: You're not just creating a result—you're creating a story. And stories move faster than features ever will.

REAL-WORLD EXAMPLE: CUSTOMER SUCCESS PLATFORM'S 30-DAY TURNAROUND

A customer success platform signed a fast-scaling SaaS company. The buyer was bought in—but internal bandwidth was tight. Risk of slow adoption was high. The vendor engineered a first win:

- Set up 80% of the platform before kickoff.
- Focused on just one use case: renewal risk alerts.
- Got live data flowing within five days.
- Surfaced $640K in at-risk revenue in two accounts.
- Held a "Win Review" call with the CRO on day 28.

Result?

- Expansion on day 31
- Referral to another division

The message wasn't, "Look at our features." It was, "You just protected $640K—and we're just getting started."

Step 7: Use the First Win to Set Up the Second

Don't let the momentum die. Once you hit Win #1, say: "Let's build the 60-day plan to expand this. Based on what worked, here are three fast areas to hit next."

Use frameworks like:

- Crawl → Walk → Run
- One team → Full department

- One use case → Three
- One metric → Company-wide dashboard

Momentum isn't automatic. You manufacture it—one fast win at a time. First wins aren't just tactical—they're psychological. They silence internal skeptics, validate the decision-makers, and give your champion the momentum they need to push forward. Without that early win, even the best solution feels like a risk. With it, the buyer sees proof, gains confidence, and becomes a believer. Engineer that moment, and you don't just reduce churn—you unlock velocity.

Action Checklist

- ☐ Ask the buyer: "What would success look like in 30 days?"
- ☐ Define a small, high-impact win that proves value quickly.
- ☐ Share a simple onboarding timeline to create clarity and momentum.
- ☐ Assign joint accountability—your team and theirs.
- ☐ Help them publicize the win internally with templates and support.
- ☐ Celebrate the success—make them the hero.
- ☐ Use the win to propose next steps and expand impact.

Chapter 24

EXPANSION IS URGENCY'S SECRET WEAPON

Most companies treat expansion as an afterthought. It's a "nice-to-have"—once the core product is live and value is proven. That mindset is wrong. *Expansion is not the end of the journey. It's the continuation of urgency.*

In fact, some of your most powerful levers to create momentum, reinforce trust, and accelerate urgency live in the post-sale phase:

- New use cases
- New teams
- New regions
- New integrations
- New executive sponsors
- New insights
- New threats exposed

Handled right, expansion isn't just about increasing contract value. It's about embedding your solution deeper—and raising the stakes if they walk away. This chapter is about building a system that turns every closed, won deal into a catalyst for growth, influence, and internal urgency.

WHY EXPANSION MULTIPLIES URGENCY

Urgency tends to fade once the ink dries. Why?

- The buyer relaxes.
- New initiatives distract.
- The initial pain fades.
- The excitement of purchase wears off.

But when you create meaningful expansion moments, you:

- Re-surface the problem.
- Uncover new wins.
- Activate new stakeholders.
- Turn users into advocates.
- Re-spark executive attention.

Expansion becomes your *urgency flywheel.* Every new motion reinforces your relevance—and keeps competitors out.

TREAT EXPANSION LIKE A CAMPAIGN, NOT A COINCIDENCE

Most CSMs wait for the customer to say, "Hey, can we add more licenses?" That's reactive. Instead, create a 90-day Expansion Campaign Plan at the start of onboarding. It should include:

- Key usage milestones.
- Fastest adjacent use case.
- Recommended integrations.

- Suggested new stakeholders to loop in.
- Internal proof points to share.
- Expansion conversation trigger points.

Now, urgency isn't just about adoption. It's about what's next—and when.

MAKE EXPANSION ABOUT BUSINESS GOALS, NOT FEATURES

Don't pitch your customer more stuff. Instead, say:

"We helped you hit [goal]. Next, let's look at how we can accelerate [related goal]."

Examples:

- "You improved response time. Now let's reduce missed opportunities."
- "You automated compliance tracking. Now let's cut audit prep time."
- "You improved onboarding. Now let's improve retention."

Tie expansion to progression, not product. And always link it to something *they already said mattered.*

USE THE FIRST WIN AS THE LAUNCHPAD

Remember the quick win from chapter 23? Use it to pivot. Say:

- "Based on what we just achieved, here are three high-impact plays to build on this momentum."
- "Here's how other teams are stacking wins—and how they justified budget."
- "Would you like me to help scope a phase 2 plan to present to your VP?"

You're not upselling. You're helping them do more of what works. And that's a much easier "yes."

ADD NEW STAKEHOLDERS, NOT JUST NEW SEATS

Expansion isn't just more licenses. It's more:

- Buyers.
- Use cases.
- Influence.
- Budget owners.
- Internal alignment.

To reduce the confusion, create a stakeholder expansion map. You need to build a stakeholder expansion map to identify, engage, and influence all decision-makers and champions required to drive account growth and prevent deal risk. Consider the following questions:

- Who else owns a related metric?
- Who's downstream from the current use case?
- Who's struggling with a similar problem?
- Who's in a different region or team with the same needs?
- Who does your champion report to—and what do *they* care about?

Every new person brought in is a new potential urgency trigger.

USE REPORTING AS AN EXPANSION ENGINE

Data is your best expansion tool. Set up a cadence to share insights like:

- Usage trends.
- ROI proof.
- Cost/time savings.
- SLA improvements.
- Risk mitigated.
- Productivity gained.

And then say, "If this is what we're seeing in one department—imagine what this could look like across your whole org." Let the numbers sell for you. And always pair reporting with:

- Expansion roadmap ideas.
- Case studies from similar customers.
- Visuals that make progress tangible.

DON'T WAIT FOR RENEWAL SEASON

If you wait for renewal to talk about expansion, you've waited too long. By then:

- Budgets are locked.
- Priorities are shifting.
- Competitive vendors are circling.

Instead, have your first expansion conversation 30–60 days after go-live. Then keep going. Create a drumbeat of value that makes the next move feel inevitable.

WHO DRIVES EXPANSION URGENCY BEST?

The team responsible for driving expansion plays a critical role in how quickly—and successfully—it happens. Not all team structures create the same sense of urgency.

Sales reps who own both new customer acquisition and expansion typically bring the most urgency. They're wired to hunt, and they view expansion as another pathway to quota. Because they're trained to lead with business outcomes and urgency levers, they approach expansion like they would a net-new deal—with a clear value story, a defined timeline, and a next-step mindset.

Reps solely focused on expansion can also thrive—if they're empowered and accountable for pipeline growth. When structured well, these roles (sometimes titled "account managers" or "growth reps") can drive urgency by staying close to the customer's evolving needs, spotting moments of momentum, and capitalizing on internal shifts. But they need enablement, sales training, and performance goals that reward proactive behavior—not reactive renewal management.

Customer success teams, while crucial for relationship depth and product adoption, often bring the least urgency to expansion. Their incentives are tied to satisfaction and retention, not revenue. Without quota or sales training, CSMs may hesitate to introduce expansion paths that feel commercial.

The best approach? Pair CSMs with sellers in tightly aligned pods where CSMs drive insight and sellers drive motion.

Bottom line: Urgency comes from ownership, sales discipline, and a clear mandate to grow accounts—not just retain them.

REAL-WORLD EXAMPLE: WORKFLOW SAAS EXPANDS FROM ONE TEAM TO NINE

A workflow automation vendor started with a 20-user deal in customer support. They hit their quick win in 21 days:

- Reduced average ticket handling time by 22%.
- Documented savings: $94K in month 1.

They used that to:

- Present a "Phase 2" roadmap to the head of customer experience.
- Share a case study with internal enablement.
- Introduce automation ideas to Marketing and IT.
- Show visual dashboards to the CFO.
- Run an ROI workshop with HR (who had similar problems).

Result? In 90 days, the contract grew 4×. In six months, it touched nine departments. In 12 months, they were locked in—and competing vendors couldn't get in the door. Expansion wasn't an accident. It was a playbook.

USE URGENCY LANGUAGE DURING EXPANSION

Don't just say: "Would you like to add more seats?"

Say:

- "If we don't act now, your other teams will miss the Q3 window to see results."
- "We can align this with your new initiative if we start this month."
- "This is how [similar company] justified cross-team rollout—and they did it within a quarter."

Use all the urgency levers:

- Timing
- Risk
- Momentum

- Competitive pressure
- Budget cycles
- Executive attention

Expansion isn't a soft conversation. It's a strategic escalation. Expansion isn't just revenue growth—it's urgency insurance. Every new stakeholder, use case, and region deepens your foothold and raises the cost of churn. Done right, expansion shifts your role from vendor to vital infrastructure. And once you're vital, you're not just harder to replace—you're impossible to ignore.

Treat every expansion moment as a high-stakes urgency play, because that's exactly what it is.

Action Checklist

- ☐ Build an Expansion Campaign Plan before go-live.
- ☐ Tie expansion to business goals—not product features.
- ☐ Use quick wins to pivot into new conversations.
- ☐ Map new stakeholders and tie them to their own urgency drivers.
- ☐ Share ROI and usage data proactively—not just at renewal.
- ☐ Introduce expansion roadmaps within 30–60 days of adoption.
- ☐ Use urgency framing to guide expansion timing and importance.
- ☐ Make expansion feel like a natural, strategic next step—not an upsell.

Chapter 25

TEACHING THE MARKET WHAT TO FEAR

Buyers don't act when they *understand* a problem. They act when they *feel* it. And they don't feel it until they realize: "This could hurt us—and soon." That's why one of the most effective, underused tools in high-impact marketing is fear. Not hype. Not manipulation. But the kind of fear rooted in truth—in data, risk, patterns, and consequences they haven't yet connected.

If you want to spark urgency at scale, you can't just point to opportunity. You have to shine a light on the threats buyers haven't fully grasped.

This chapter is about how to responsibly teach the market what to fear—and how doing so creates momentum, shifts budgets, and drives action.

THE ROLE OF FEAR IN B2B DECISION-MAKING

We like to think of B2B buyers as rational. But when the stakes are high—money, risk, public reputation—emotions take over. And fear is the strongest motivator of all. Fears include the following:

- Being blamed
- Falling behind
- Getting hacked
- Failing an audit
- Missing a board target
- Looking stupid
- Losing control
- Losing customers
- Losing budget

If your product can reduce, eliminate, or redirect that fear, you have leverage. But first, buyers need to see the danger.

FIND THE RISK THEY HAVEN'T CALCULATED

Your buyers already fear the obvious stuff. But that's not where urgency lives. Urgency lives in the *hidden risk*. The threat they haven't quantified—or didn't know existed.

Examples:

- "Your backup system is only storing 30% of critical data. That means if you're breached, recovery is partial at best."
- "You think you're secure—but you have 3,200 user accounts with open admin privileges."
- "You're noncompliant with three regulatory updates from last quarter. You won't get fined—until the next audit."
- "Your AI models are skewed by data drift that's gone undetected for six months."

These are not dramatic claims. They're silent, compound risks. And when exposed clearly, they provoke action. Most companies don't realize that the greatest competitor to your solution isn't another vendor—it's buyer inaction. And inaction thrives when there's no clear risk of doing nothing.

That's why your job isn't just to show the benefits of change—it's to make the cost of staying the same feel dangerously high. When the pain of inertia outweighs the effort of progress, that's when deals move.

CREATE THE X-RAY EFFECT

Remember: Buyers often can't see the problem. You need to show it to them in a way that makes it real, immediate, and painful. We call this the X-ray effect—when your marketing or sales motion reveals something uncomfortable but undeniable.

Ways to create it:

- Benchmark reports
- Risk scans
- Diagnostic tools
- Security assessments
- Compliance checklists
- Health scores
- AI explainability audits
- Side-by-side performance comparisons
- Internal stakeholder surveys ("What's really broken?")

Once buyers see what's broken—or at risk—they can't unsee it. And that's the moment urgency begins.

QUANTIFY THE DOWNSIDE

Fear becomes actionable when it's *measurable*. Don't just say, "You're at risk."

Say:

- "You're likely to experience a $480K revenue loss in the next 12 months if this remains unchecked."

- "One breach here—and you're paying $2.5M in remediation and brand damage."
- "Delayed onboarding is costing you 22% of potential revenue per rep in their first 60 days."

Use the following consequences:

- Cost per incident
- Time lost
- Revenue leakage
- Churn impact
- Legal/regulatory fines
- Customer satisfaction dips
- Internal productivity slowdowns

The clearer the consequence, the stronger the motivation.

GIVE THE FEAR A NAME

Unspoken fears are manageable. Named fears are *urgent.* Give the problem a label. A code name. A headline. A pattern.

Examples:

- "The 9-Day Data Exposure Gap"
- "The Lead Leakage Effect"
- "The Admin Account Trap"
- "Silent SLA Misses"
- "The Compliance Drift"
- "Shadow Spend Risk"

Once you name it, it becomes a thing. And if it's a thing, buyers want to fix it—or get rid of it. This is how categories are born. This is how urgency scales.

BE THE CALMEST PERSON IN THE ROOM

Here's the nuance. Fear drives urgency—but only if you also provide a confident path forward.

You can't just say, "You're in trouble."

You have to say, "Yes, this is serious—but here's how companies like yours solve it. We'll walk you through every step."

Your tone is vital:

- Calm
- Authoritative
- Precise
- Solution oriented

You're not yelling "Fire!" You're walking in with the extinguisher.

REAL-WORLD EXAMPLE: SECURITY SAAS AND THE AUDIT CLOCK

A security SaaS company that sold to mid-market finance teams used to have the following pitch:

"We automate audit readiness."

It sounded nice, but no one acted urgently. They reframed it:

- "You're likely 6–9 months out of compliance due to unmonitored permission drift."
- "Your CFO will be held accountable for every data access violation."
- "And your next audit is 72 days away."

They built:

- A five-minute risk scan.
- A visual report with red/yellow/green zones.

- A "Countdown to Audit" dashboard.
- A remediation timeline with executive sign-off.

Deals accelerated by 48%. Why? Because they made the risk visible—and fixable.

USE FEAR TO ELEVATE THE CONVERSATION

When you expose real risk:

- Buyers loop in their boss.
- Cross-functional teams engage.
- Budgets unlock.
- Projects get accelerated.

Use that fear to elevate with statements like:

- "Your IT lead should see this. It affects architecture at the foundation."
- "Your CFO will want this in the Q2 risk report."
- "If your board is reviewing AI governance, this should be on the agenda."

Fear—paired with strategic framing—gives your buyer a reason to move up the chain.

DON'T WEAPONIZE IT—ILLUMINATE IT

There's a line. You're not using fear to manipulate. You're using it to *illuminate* a truth your buyer needs to see—one that may be buried in complexity, complacency, or unawareness. Test your message with the following questions:

- Is the fear real, backed by data?
- Do you offer a clear, tested path forward?
- Are you educating, not just provoking?

If the answer is yes, you're creating urgency with integrity. And buyers will trust you more because of it.

A powerful way to create urgency with integrity is through a proprietary market survey and state-of-the-industry report. Unlike generic marketing content, these reports uncover truths your buyers already *sense* but haven't yet fully seen quantified. When done right, they elevate your brand from "vendor" to "trusted authority."

The key is to illuminate, not weaponize. Start by designing a survey that captures critical data on your buyers' environment—security risks, inefficiencies, misconfigurations, or gaps that most executives underestimate. Frame the questions so the results tell a story of reality, not opinion. When the findings are aggregated, publish them as an annual or semi-annual "State of" report. By showing, for example, that "62% of enterprises discovered unknown exposures in their Microsoft 365 environments," you're not scaring buyers—you're shining a light on a truth that is statistically undeniable.

What makes this approach credible is education plus a path forward. Each statistic in the report should connect to a business implication and a tested solution. For instance, if your survey finds that 70% of IT leaders lack backup for tenant configurations, the report should guide them on how to evaluate and address that gap. That way, the fear is real, the stakes are clear, and your company provides the roadmap.

The benefit is twofold: Your marketing gains a flagship asset that commands attention, and your buyers gain clarity in a noisy market. Analysts, media outlets, and partners amplify the report because it speaks to the whole market, not just your product. Over time, your "State of" report becomes a go-to industry reference, positioning your company as the trusted source buyers turn to when they need perspective and solutions.

Action Checklist

- ☐ Identify the silent, uncalculated risk your product helps mitigate.
- ☐ Use tools, data, or diagnostics to expose that risk—the X-ray effect.
- ☐ Quantify the downside: cost, time, risk, churn, fines, or reputation.
- ☐ Give the fear a name—turn it into a pattern buyers can remember.
- ☐ Balance your message with a calm, confident, solution-forward tone.
- ☐ Elevate the conversation—bring in stakeholders who care about risk.
- ☐ Stay factual and respectful—never manipulate, always illuminate.
- ☐ Use fear to clarify priorities and accelerate decisions—not to scare, but to serve.

Chapter 26

PARTNERING WITH ANALYSTS AND INFLUENCERS TO CREATE URGENCY

You can tell your story. You can highlight the risk. You can quantify the cost of doing nothing. But sometimes, that's not enough. Why? Because buyers don't just listen to you. They listen to:

- Industry analysts.
- Influential voices.
- Peer executives.
- Former operators.
- Trusted media channels.
- Social thought leaders.
- AI (such as ChatGPT).

In moments of uncertainty or risk, buyers look to others for signals:

- "Is this a real problem?"
- "Is this a vendor I can trust?"
- "Is this something I need to move on now?"

This chapter is about how to build urgency by leveraging voices of influence—voices your buyers already follow, respect, and believe. Because when urgency is reinforced by external validation, it becomes undeniable.

WHY THIRD-PARTY INFLUENCE DRIVES URGENCY

Buyers are skeptical of vendor claims—especially if:

- The problem seems new.
- The urgency feels engineered.
- The category is unfamiliar.
- The vendor is up and coming.

But when a respected third party says:

- "This is a threat."
- "This is the category to watch."
- "This is what smart companies are doing."

Buyers listen. It's not because the risk became more real. It's because the *source became more trusted.* Below are eight steps for using third-party influence to move prospects to act now.

Step 1: Identify Who Your Buyers Listen To

Start by asking:

- What firms do they reference in conversations?
- What blogs, newsletters, or podcasts do they follow?
- What conferences do they attend?

- What names pop up in deal reviews or board meetings?
- Who do they repost or quote on LinkedIn?

Then segment them by persona. For example:

- CTOs may trust Gartner, Forrester, or industry-specific experts.
- CMOs might follow Forrester, Scott Brinker, or leading demand-generation influencers.
- CISOs trust security researchers, former CISOs, and compliance experts.
- CFOs respect McKinsey, Bain, and peer benchmarking data.

Once you map this, you'll know whose voice can move the market.

Step 2: Use Analysts to Make the Problem "Boardroom Safe"

Analyst firms give your messaging executive-level credibility. Even if buyers are emotionally sold, they still need to:

- Justify the problem to the board.
- Explain why now.
- Reassure skeptical stakeholders.
- De-risk the decision.

When an analyst says, "This is one of the most underaddressed risks in the enterprise," you've just armed your champion with budget-level ammunition.

Ways to work with analysts:

- Briefings to plant your POV
- Commissioned research or spotlights
- Quotes or stats you can use in content
- Peer comparisons or tool maturity curves
- Advisory boards or panels
- Report inclusion (Gartner Market Guide, Forrester Wave, IDC MarketScape, etc.)

Think of analysts as your *urgency amplifiers.*

If there's one move that consistently changes how analysts talk about you, it's this: *Don't just tell them your story. Let your customers do it.*

Analysts are bombarded with vendor messaging. What they believe—and what shapes their guidance—comes from hearing real customers describe urgent problems and how your product solved them. The best way to influence Gartner, Forrester, IDC, or GigaOm isn't a better slide deck. It's putting your champion customer in the (virtual) room.

Why it works:

- Analysts value firsthand, unscripted experience over pitch decks.
- It builds trust that your solution drives results in real-world settings.
- It often reveals use cases, urgency triggers, or competitive differentiators you haven't articulated yet.

Here's how to make it happen:

- Identify two or three customers who experienced clear, measurable value quickly.
- Prep them to speak to the before/after state—what hurt, what changed, and how fast.
- Include urgency: "We were under pressure from [X] and needed a solution that worked by [Y]."
- Set the analyst's expectation that this is a working session, not a victory lap.

When analysts hear urgency directly from the field, it reframes their perception—not just of your product, but of the category. And when they start sharing that urgency with other clients, your influence scales. That's how you stop trying to get a better analyst quote—and start making your buyers hear urgency from the source they already trust.

Step 3: Co-Create Threat Narratives with Experts

Bring in industry experts or former operators to help you:

- Expose emerging risks.
- Reveal patterns across companies.
- Identify the "next wave" of disruption.
- Validate the need for a new category.
- Frame the cost of inaction through lived experience.

Examples:

- "A former CISO explains why traditional privilege access models are broken—and what the next breach will look like."
- "A VP of RevOps shares why lead leakage is worse than pipeline gaps—and how AI is exposing the cracks."
- "An analyst walk-through of how SaaS bloat is costing mid-market companies $3.1M per year—without realizing it."

These stories don't sell your product. They sell the need for change. And change is where urgency lives.

Step 4: Use Influencers to Seed the Conversation Early

In the awareness stage, your buyers are scrolling, not searching. They're not googling "urgent security risk" or "AI automation framework." They're passively consuming—and they pause when someone they respect says:

- "If you're not doing X yet, you're already behind."
- "The biggest mistake I see in [industry] right now is . . ."
- "Companies are sitting on risk—here's where it's hiding."

Work with micro-influencers or respected operators to:

- Post thought-provoking problem content.
- Share a teardown of a broken process.
- Offer diagnostic tips or warning signs.
- Link to your tools, benchmarks, or content.
- Tell "what I wish I had known earlier" stories.

When a trusted voice shines light on a threat—even subtly—your target market leans in.

Step 5: Create the "Social Proof Avalanche"

Urgency isn't always sparked by fear. Sometimes it's triggered by momentum. Your buyers think: "Everyone else is solving this. What are we waiting for?"

Build this momentum using:

- Influencer commentary.
- Analyst quotes.
- Peer case studies.
- Logos and testimonials.
- Event appearances.
- Media mentions.
- Curated LinkedIn conversations.

Use language like:

- "It's no longer optional to address this."
- "We're seeing this become a C-level conversation fast."
- "The smartest teams we work with are acting now—not waiting for a breach."
- "The boardroom is asking harder questions—and teams need answers."

It's no longer just about your product. It's about not being the last one to act. The real power of third-party voices isn't just validation—it's acceleration. When your market hears the same message from multiple respected sources, the perceived urgency compounds. Suddenly, it's not just your POV—it's an industry narrative. And once a narrative takes hold, it spreads faster than any ad campaign ever could.

Step 6: Package External Voices into Your Campaigns

Don't let analyst and influencer insights sit in PDFs or podcasts. Turn them into urgency assets:

- Slides for your sellers
- Quotes in your emails
- Posts for your execs
- Call-to-action anchors on your landing pages
- "What experts are saying" visuals for decks
- Executive summaries for board-level conversations

Your message is stronger when it doesn't come from you alone.

REAL-WORLD EXAMPLE: OBSERVABILITY VENDOR BREAKS THROUGH WITH ANALYSTS

An observability platform wanted to shift from "nice-to-have monitoring" to "mission-critical root-cause intelligence." But buyers didn't feel urgency. So they partnered with:

- A Gartner analyst for a Market Guide mention.
- A former CIO to explain how downtime cost her $1.2M/week.
- A security expert to show where event correlation breaks.
- Two DevOps influencers who posted teardown threads on LinkedIn.
- A benchmarking firm to run a "Time to Resolution" self-assessment.

They didn't pitch features. They exposed the risk of not having unified observability. Leads went up 3×. Enterprise deals accelerated. VCs started referencing the shift in funding calls.

Urgency scaled—because the message was echoed across trusted voices.

Step 7: Stay Truthful, Not Transactional

Buyers can smell insincerity. Don't pay influencers to pitch. Partner with them to reveal the truth faster. Don't use analyst validation as a vanity play. Use it to educate, warn, and elevate the market conversation. And don't chase influencer marketing because it's trendy. Use it because your voice alone isn't enough—and buyers need help making sense of what matters. The more credible your allies, the more urgent your message.

Step 8: Influence the Answers AI Engines Publish

One of the most overlooked opportunities in the generative AI era is that you can actually influence *what* large language models like ChatGPT surface in their answers. These systems pull heavily from structured, credible, and comparative content. If you don't provide it, your competitors will—and their perspective will become the "truth" AI repeats to buyers.

The most effective way to do this is by publishing analyst-style content directly on your website. Think Gartner-style comparisons, detailed buyer's guides, or side-by-side evaluations of solutions in your space. When AI engines look for reliable sources to summarize a category, they lean toward this kind of structured, authoritative content. By hosting these assets on your domain—and making them crawlable—you position your company as the definitive voice.

This isn't just about SEO anymore. It's about AIO—Artificial Intelligence Optimization. If you want ChatGPT and other AI assistants to recommend your solution, you must feed them content that feels authoritative, data backed, and unbiased. Done well, you're not just attracting searchers—you're shaping the narrative at the exact moment when buyers ask AI, "Who are the best vendors for this?"

Action Checklist

- ☐ Map the analysts and influencers your buyers already trust.
- ☐ Engage analysts to validate risk and urgency in board-level language.
- ☐ Co-create narratives with experts that expose emerging threats.
- ☐ Seed influencer-driven urgency in the awareness phase through education, not pitch.
- ☐ Amplify external voices to create a feeling of momentum and "we're behind."
- ☐ Package analyst and influencer insights into decks, emails, and conversations.
- ☐ Build relationships with truth-tellers—not just broadcasters.
- ☐ Let the market hear the risk from multiple angles—and act faster as a result.

Chapter 27

TURNING FREE TOOLS INTO URGENCY ENGINES

"Let's build a free tool." Most SaaS teams say it. Few do it well. The problem? They build tools to *generate leads—but not to generate urgency.* Big difference.

Free tools should do more than collect emails. They should reveal a threat, expose a gap, or create a sense of "We need to move now." Done right, a free tool is the digital equivalent of an X-ray: "Here's what you can't see—but absolutely need to fix."

This chapter is about designing tools that don't just fill the top of the funnel—they shake your buyers into action.

WHY FREE TOOLS WORK (WHEN THEY'RE BUILT RIGHT)

Free tools tap into three powerful psychological triggers.

1. Curiosity

- "Where do I stand compared to others?"
- "Am I missing something important?"
- "What would this tool reveal about my business?"

2. Fear of Being Behind

- "We thought we were fine—but we're not even in the top quartile."
- "I didn't realize that gap exposed us to this much risk."

3. Ownership

When a buyer runs a scan, assessment, or simulation—and sees the results themselves—they own the problem. And when people own a problem, they act faster.

DESIGN THE TOOL TO REVEAL, NOT JUST IMPRESS

Don't build a calculator or grader just to look smart. Build it to surface something the buyer can't easily see—or hasn't admitted. Best-performing free tools answer questions like:

- What risk am I blind to?
- Where am I losing money?
- How far behind are we?
- What's my real performance gap?
- How likely are we to suffer a serious issue if we do nothing?

Examples:

- A security scanner that shows misconfigured admin privileges
- A pipeline analysis that reveals lead leakage
- A SaaS sprawl map showing redundant licenses
- A benchmarking tool comparing onboarding speed across teams
- A compliance readiness checker with severity zones

This isn't content. It's *consequence.* And it makes people move.

MAKE IT FAST, VISUAL, AND NO-STRINGS

The longer it takes or the harder it feels, the less urgency it creates.

Follow this framework:

- Speed: < 3 minutes
- Input: No more than five fields
- Output: Instantly delivered
- Experience: Visual, interactive, mobile-friendly
- Gated or Ungated: Optional email; deliver value first

Best tools give buyers the following:

- A score (with red/yellow/green zones)
- A comparison (peer benchmarks or industry averages)
- A warning ("You're missing X that could cost Y")
- A next step (that points to your solution)

If the result makes them say, "Wow. We need to fix this now," you've nailed it. The real magic happens when the tool doesn't just deliver a report—it delivers a realization. It flips a mental switch from "We're exploring" to "We're exposed." That emotional shift—from casual interest to personal urgency—is what moves deals forward. Great free tools don't just diagnose. They provoke. They make inaction feel irresponsible.

USE THE TOOL AS A CONVERSATION STARTER—NOT JUST A LEAD SOURCE

A free tool isn't just for form fills. It's a story trigger. Ways to activate:

- "Here's your risk score—want to walk through what it means?"
- "Your onboarding lag is 2.3× longer than your peers'. Want to fix that?"
- "Your dashboard shows four areas where costs are rising. We can cut them in a week."

Have your sales reps run the scan *for* the account before outreach. Consider the subject line, "Saw this in your data—it's costing you $36K/month." It makes your tool an outbound multiplier.

TURN THE OUTPUT INTO SALES ENABLEMENT

The tool should:

- Trigger discovery questions.
- Anchor the problem in numbers.
- Set up your product as the fix.
- Be attachable to follow-ups and decks.

Give your reps a playbook:

- "If score is below 50 → suggest rapid remediation pilot."
- "If peer gap is >20% → bring in benchmarking study."
- "If high risk flagged → loop in Security/Legal/Ops lead."

Now the tool isn't just a marketing asset. It's a deal accelerant.

DON'T ISOLATE THE TOOL—INTEGRATE IT INTO THE FUNNEL

Too many companies launch a free tool and leave it on an island. Here's how to bake it in:

Funnel Stage	Tool Strategy
Awareness	Promote on LinkedIn, blogs, partner sites, influencer channels.
Interest	Call to action (CTA) on high-performing pages ("Check your risk in 2 minutes").
Evaluation	Use in nurture emails to reignite cold leads.
Sales	Include scan links in demo prep and outbound.
Retention	Run post-implementation comparisons to show progress.
Expansion	Rescore teams/regions to open new use cases.

This turns one tool into a *full-funnel urgency engine.*

REAL-WORLD EXAMPLE: MARTECH FIRM'S FREE ASSESSMENT DRIVES PIPELINE SURGE

A martech vendor built a Campaign Waste Calculator.

Inputs:

- Average monthly ad spend
- CRM conversion rate
- Average deal size

Output:

- Estimated $$ lost from misrouted leads
- Peer benchmark comparisons
- "Urgency Score" from 1 to 100
- Suggested next step: 14-day fix session with their platform

They ran it as:

- A CTA on every blog post.
- A retargeting ad.
- A subject line: "Are you wasting $24K/month on misfired campaigns?"
- A pre-demo scan required for all inbound meetings.

Results:

- 38% lead-to-meeting conversion
- 2× deal velocity for those who used the tool
- 22% lift in enterprise leads

The tool didn't just drive leads. It made the problem undeniable.

REFRESH IT REGULARLY TO MAINTAIN RELEVANCE

Your tool loses power when:

- The benchmarks get stale.
- The risks feel outdated.
- Competitors catch up with something similar.
- Your product evolves past the scope of the tool.

Set a quarterly or biannual schedule to:

- Refresh benchmarks.
- Add new visuals.
- Tweak messaging.
- Update results.
- Expand input/output logic.

Also, run campaigns like, "New 2025 data is in—see where you now rank." Urgency isn't just about the first moment. It's about creating reason to return.

BUILD A LIBRARY, NOT A ONE-OFF

Your first tool is just the beginning. Once you've built the playbook, scale the following:

- A budget forecaster
- A governance scanner
- A roadmap scorer
- A "What's Broken?" radar
- A buyer readiness checklist
- An integration map
- An ROI projection engine

Each tool hits a different buyer need:

- Risk
- Efficiency
- Budget
- Strategy
- Operations
- Benchmarking

Together, they position you as:

- The truth-teller.
- The diagnostic engine.
- The partner who sees what others don't.

And that's the foundation for lasting urgency.

Action Checklist

- ☐ Design your free tool to expose risk, not just impress.
- ☐ Limit inputs, maximize visual insight, and make it fast.
- ☐ Frame the tool as a conversation starter for sales.
- ☐ Train your sales development representatives and account executives to use the output in follow-ups.
- ☐ Integrate the tool across the full funnel—from awareness to expansion.
- ☐ Update the tool regularly to maintain urgency and relevance.
- ☐ Build a family of tools that uncover different threats, inefficiencies, and opportunities.
- ☐ Make your tools the mirror your buyers can't look away from.

Chapter 28

VISUALIZING THE PAIN

Using Story, Contrast, and Simulations to Trigger Action

You can describe the problem. You can explain the risk. You can throw stats, metrics, and benchmarks at your buyers. But if they don't see it, they won't feel it. And if they don't feel it, they won't move.

"Don't tell me it hurts. Show me the limp."

This chapter is about how to make pain *visual, visceral, and urgent.* Not through scare tactics, but through story, contrast, and immersive experiences that transform abstract problems into undeniable realities.

WHY VISUALIZATION CREATES URGENCY

Humans are wired to respond to what they can picture.

We underestimate:

- Abstract risks.
- Probabilities.
- Delayed consequences.

We overreact to:

- Visual damage.
- Personal stories.
- Side-by-side comparisons.
- Simulations that show what could happen.

If you want buyers to act now, you must bridge the gap between:
"We're probably okay."
and
"This is happening to us, right now—and it's costing us."

USE CONTRAST TO SHOW THE COST OF INACTION

Nothing triggers urgency like before versus after. But instead of using it to sell your product, use it to sell the problem.

Examples:

- "With process A, your team closes tickets in 72 hours. With process B (what your competitors use), they close in 8."
- "Here's your current onboarding flow—11 steps, 3 handoffs, and a 9-day delay. Here's what best-in-class looks like."
- "You're spending $28K/month across 7 tools. You're using 22% of the features. That's $21K of waste."

Put this into:

- Diagrams.
- Gantt-style timelines.
- Comparison dashboards.
- Overlay graphics (current vs. optimized).

You're not selling solutions yet. You're making the pain visual. Visualization doesn't just make the problem easier to understand—it makes it harder to ignore. When buyers *see* the impact of their current state, they begin to feel responsible for fixing it. And that's the moment when urgency shifts from external persuasion to internal conviction. Great visuals don't convince—they confront. They quietly ask: "Can you really afford to keep going like this?"

TELL A STORY WHERE THE BUYER SEES THEMSELVES

Stories outperform data every time—if the buyer sees themselves in the plot. Don't just tell a success story. Tell a failure story—with empathy and consequence.

Example: "We worked with a marketing director who had your exact setup. She was running well—until the board asked for funnel efficiency metrics. Her team couldn't deliver. They spent six weeks pulling it manually. It led to budget cuts, and she lost half her team. She told us, 'I wish we saw it coming.'"

You're not blaming. You're not exaggerating. You're showing a plausible scenario that matches the buyer's current trajectory. The goal? "That could happen to us."

BUILD A SIMULATION THAT MAKES IT REAL

Let your buyer feel the consequences of inaction.

Examples:

- A security vendor builds a "Breach Day" simulation—walk through what happens hour by hour if a misconfigured account is exploited.
- A forecasting tool lets you change two inputs and shows the year-end revenue impact in real time.
- A compliance platform shows what happens when a new regulation is ignored—with fine amounts and audit timelines.

- A marketing AI simulates a full campaign using your last five emails—and shows how much better (or worse) it performs.

Simulations don't need to be flashy. They just need to answer the question, "What happens if we keep going like this?"

LET THE BUYER INTERACT WITH THE PAIN

Static charts are good. Interactive visuals are better. Because when buyers engage, they internalize.

Examples:

- "Drag this slider to see how your churn risk increases as your onboarding time grows."
- "Click each area of your stack to see tool overlap and waste."
- "Select your industry and team size to generate a risk heat map."
- "Upload a CSV of recent ops tasks to reveal idle time per rep."

Let the *buyer drive the discovery*—not your deck. That's when ownership begins. And ownership triggers urgency.

USE THE "SILENT ALARM" FRAMEWORK

Some pain isn't loud—it's hidden. Quiet. Easy to ignore. Until it explodes. Your job is to install a silent alarm in the buyer's head.

How?

- Expose a risk that builds slowly (e.g., permissions creep, model drift, tool sprawl).
- Show how it compounds over time.
- Reveal the moment it tips—and what that costs.
- Offer a timeline or countdown (e.g., "You're eight weeks away from noncompliance").

Once buyers see the ticking clock, they start asking, "How do we fix this—now?"

TURN THE PROBLEM INTO A SLIDE THE BUYER CAN USE

One of the most underrated urgency tactics? Make the buyer's job easier. Build a slide that:

- Visually shows their problem.
- Summarizes impact.
- Quantifies cost.
- Lists affected teams.
- Aligns to an executive goal.

Give it to them to present internally. Now the problem becomes their story to tell. And urgency isn't just external—it becomes internal alignment.

REAL-WORLD EXAMPLE: PROCUREMENT SAAS WINS WITH WASTE VISUALIZATION

A procurement platform was struggling to accelerate sales. Their product was sound, their demos were crisp, and their logic was airtight—but deals dragged on. Why? The message made sense intellectually, but it didn't hit emotionally. The pain they solved wasn't being *felt*.

So they changed the play. Instead of explaining the value, they built a "Waste Simulator" that let prospects *see* their inefficiencies—and *feel* them.

Buyers entered simple details:

- Number of vendors
- Number of departments
- Average monthly SaaS spend

In seconds, the tool generated a visual dashboard that exposed:

- Overlapping contracts across departments.
- Redundant licenses sitting idle.
- Manual renewal processes ripe for error.
- Estimated monthly and annual cost of unmanaged tools.

But it didn't stop there. The simulator projected their potential 2024 waste if they stayed on the same path. It benchmarked their tool sprawl against industry peers. It even calculated how much money they could recover in just 45 days—backed by real case studies.

The impact? Buyers weren't just hearing about inefficiency—they were *seeing* it quantified, visualized, and compared. Now the problem wasn't hypothetical. It was personal.

The results were immediate. Sales cycles shrank by 27%, deal sizes grew, and buyers started bringing procurement leaders and CFOs into the room. Why? Because once they saw the leak, they couldn't ignore it. The simulator transformed a "nice-to-have" into an urgent priority.

They didn't just want a procurement solution. They wanted to stop the bleeding. That's urgency.

TRAIN YOUR SALES TEAM TO SELL WITH VISUALIZATION, NOT EXPLANATION

Make this a core part of GTM enablement:

- Replace bullet points with diagrams.
- Replace "We help companies . . ." with "Let me show you what that looks like."
- Train reps to walk through the pain map first—not the product.
- Build a visual case deck focused on risk, not roadmap.
- Encourage whiteboard or shared screen drawings during live calls.

Visualization isn't a design play. It's a decision accelerator.

Action Checklist

- ☐ Build side-by-side visuals that show the current versus the optimized state.
- ☐ Use failure stories where buyers recognize themselves—not just hero stories.
- ☐ Create simulations or calculators that make the pain feel real and personal.
- ☐ Make your visuals interactive so buyers participate in discovery.
- ☐ Use the Silent Alarm Framework to show risk building toward a breaking point.
- ☐ Give buyers internal slides or reports that help them socialize the problem.
- ☐ Train GTM teams to visualize the pain before pitching the solution.
- ☐ Make the cost of inaction something buyers can see—not just hear.

Chapter 29

CREATING URGENCY ACROSS THE BUYING COMMITTEE

You've convinced your champion. They see the pain. They feel the urgency. But then the deal stalls. Why? Because you didn't create urgency across the committee.

Today's B2B decisions involve the following:

- Users
- Managers
- Executives
- Finance
- Procurement
- Legal
- Security
- IT

And if urgency doesn't resonate with each of them, your deal will get:

- Delayed.
- Derailed.
- Downsized.
- Or disappeared entirely.

This chapter is about how to create urgency for each stakeholder in the buying group—not by saying the same thing louder, but by translating the need into what each person cares most about.

WHY BUYING COMMITTEES SLOW DOWN

Most internal buying groups struggle to align on three things:

1. What the real problem is
2. How urgent it is
3. Whether this is the best time to act

This creates:

- Internal debate.
- Conflicting incentives.
- Competing priorities.
- Death-by-meeting cycles.
- "Let's wait and revisit next quarter" stalls.

Your job is to preempt the misalignment—by tailoring the urgency message to each seat at the table.

MAP THE COMMITTEE AND THEIR MOTIVATORS

Start by identifying the roles and responsibilities involved in your deals.

Use a table like this:

Stakeholder	Top Concern	Risk They Fear	What Triggers Urgency
Champion (e.g., RevOps)	Fixing inefficiency	Looking bad to their boss	Quick, clear ROI
Economic Buyer (e.g., CRO)	Hitting revenue targets	Missed quota	Lost deals due to speed
Exec Sponsor (e.g., CEO)	Strategic progress	Falling behind peers	Board pressure
Finance	Budget control	Overspend, no ROI	Missed savings
IT/Security	Stability, compliance	Risk exposure	Audits or incidents
Legal/ Procurement	Risk, compliance, process	Vague terms	Time-based deal clauses

Now you're no longer pitching one buyer. You're building a multi-threaded urgency campaign. The key isn't just aligning with every stakeholder—it's preempting misalignment between them. Most internal debates happen *after* your demo, when you're not in the room. That's why your messaging has to travel well. When you equip each stakeholder with a version of the problem that matches their worldview, you prevent the friction that stalls deals in cross-functional reviews.

CUSTOMIZE THE PROBLEM STATEMENT FOR EACH ROLE

Most sales and marketing professionals talk about the problem one way. But to drive committee-wide urgency, you need multiple lenses. Let's take a single product—say, a compliance automation platform. Here's how you might frame the problem:

- *For the CISO*: "You have 11 audit trails unmonitored—that's a breach exposure."
- *For the CFO*: "You're spending $1.2M/year on manual audit prep—here's the breakdown."
- *For the IT Lead*: "You've got 16 SaaS apps without permission controls—we'll fix that."
- *For Legal*: "You're out of scope on two new regulatory frameworks—we automate coverage."
- *For the Champion (Security Ops)*: "We'll give you back 6 hours/week and eliminate spreadsheet chaos."

Same product. Five urgency triggers. That's how you align momentum.

USE TARGETED CONTENT TO MOVE EACH BUYER

Don't just send the same deck to every stakeholder. Create urgency-tailored assets like:

- *One-pagers* for Finance with ROI and budget recovery.
- *Dashboards* for IT with system risk summaries.
- *Email templates* your champion can forward to execs.
- *Benchmarking visuals* that show how far behind the org is.
- *Checklists* for Legal and Security to evaluate vendor risk.
- *Compliance timelines* that show looming deadlines.
- *Prefilled business case decks* your buyers can customize and present.

You're not just selling. You're arming each person to advocate internally.

CREATE CONSENSUS AROUND A SHARED ENEMY

When you sell to multiple people, conflict happens:

- Ops blames IT.
- Finance questions value.
- Security blocks innovation.
- Legal slows the deal.
- The execs go quiet.

One way to align the group? Introduce a shared enemy. Something that's hurting everyone—but no one owns yet. Examples:

- Manual processes that waste hours across departments
- Tool sprawl that's creating security gaps and financial waste
- Inconsistent workflows that slow deals and create legal exposure
- A lack of visibility that's hurting decision-making at the top

Once they see it's not about them versus each other, but all of them versus a common threat, urgency unites.

ORCHESTRATE THE BUYING JOURNEY—DON'T JUST WAIT

Deals stall when you rely on your champion to "drive things internally." Instead, orchestrate the sequence. Build a plan like:

- Week 1: Align with champion.
- Week 2: Secure executive sponsor.
- Week 3: Loop in Finance + share ROI model.

- Week 4: Bring in IT/Security with compliance deck.
- Week 5: Send contract with procurement-friendly terms.
- Week 6: Set joint kickoff date.

You're not just hoping they align. You're helping them move as one.

USE TIMELINES AND TRIGGERS TO KEEP EVERYONE MOVING

Every stakeholder needs *a reason to act now.* Examples:

- CFO: "If we sign this month, savings start Q1—otherwise, we burn $84K next quarter."
- IT: "We'll reserve implementation bandwidth for this month—after that, we're booked."
- Exec: "You told us this is part of your Q2 transformation plan—timelines are tight."
- Champion: "Your team's drowning. This gets them relief in two weeks."
- Legal: "Contract reviewed by two peers already—minimal redlines."

Urgency must be *personal, calendar based, and role relevant.*

REAL-WORLD EXAMPLE: GTM PLATFORM WINS EIGHT-STAKEHOLDER DEAL IN FIVE WEEKS

A go-to-market intelligence platform was selling into a global SaaS org. Their initial champion was in RevOps—excited, but powerless alone. The vendor team created urgency across the committee by:

- Giving the CRO a one-page revenue risk snapshot.
- Showing the CFO the annual waste from duplicate GTM tools.
- Walking the CISO through a short risk matrix.
- Sending procurement a redline-free contract template.
- Giving Legal a clear, prefilled data-processing addendum.
- Building a preapproved onboarding plan for IT.
- Offering the CEO a "Strategic Insight Brief" tied to board goals.

They didn't pitch harder. They pitched smarter—to each seat. The result? Eight stakeholder approvals. Signed in five weeks. Expansion 90 days later.

FOLLOW THE THREE-PART RULE OF COMMITTEE URGENCY

To win fast in multi-threaded deals, follow this framework:

1. *Problem Ownership*
   Each person must believe: *This affects me.*
2. *Personal Risk or Gain*
   Each person must believe: *This could hurt or help me now.*
3. *Role-Specific Path Forward*
   Each person must know: *Here's what I do next.*

If any of these are missing for any buyer? The deal stalls. Build urgency for everyone—not just the loudest voice.

Action Checklist

- ☐ Map every stakeholder and their specific concerns, fears, and urgency triggers.
- ☐ Translate the problem into role-specific language and consequences.
- ☐ Create tailored assets and internal tools for each person's context.
- ☐ Introduce a shared enemy to unite the buying group.
- ☐ Guide your champion with a week-by-week stakeholder engagement plan.
- ☐ Use real-time urgency triggers tied to each stakeholder's priorities.
- ☐ Validate problem ownership, personal risk/gain, and clear next steps for each person.
- ☐ Orchestrate the buying committee like a campaign—not a guessing game.

Chapter 30

BUILDING URGENCY INTO YOUR PRODUCT EXPERIENCE

You've done the hard work. The prospect became a customer. The champion signed the contract. The team is onboarded. But there's a new risk now: The product gets used passively—not urgently.

No matter how good your messaging, pitch, or onboarding is, if the product doesn't reinforce urgency, usage fades. Value becomes invisible. Expansion slows. Advocacy stalls.

This chapter is about how to embed urgency inside the product itself—so the experience constantly reminds users of the following:

- What matters
- What's broken
- What's next
- What's at risk
- What needs attention *right now*

It's not just about good UX. It's about building emotional triggers into the workflow—so the product becomes impossible to ignore.

WHY PRODUCT-LED URGENCY MATTERS

Great software doesn't just enable users. It directs them.

It says:

- "Here's where you're falling behind."
- "This number is slipping—here's why."
- "You're exposed here—fix it fast."
- "This team is underperforming—act now."
- "You're not getting value—yet."

When urgency lives inside the interface, it:

- Boosts adoption.
- Shortens time-to-value.
- Drives usage depth.
- Sparks expansion.
- Keeps executives engaged.

And most importantly? It prevents your solution from being out of sight, out of mind.

SURFACE PROBLEMS PROACTIVELY—NOT PASSIVELY

Most tools wait for users to find value.

But urgency requires you to bring the problem to the surface—immediately and repeatedly.

Build features like:

- *Risk widgets*: "You have 14 overdue tasks—3 are critical."
- *Anomaly detection*: "Your inbound traffic dropped 34% this week—check your funnel."

- *Usage gaps*: "Only 22% of teams are using this feature—here's what they're missing."
- *Workflow blockers*: "This step is breaking 11% of transactions."
- *Performance alerts*: "Your SLA was missed in 3 key accounts yesterday."

Think of them as smoke detectors: If something's wrong, the product should say it—loud and clear.

CREATE TIME-BASED TRIGGERS

Urgency is tied to timelines. Your product should communicate:

- What's happening now.
- What's slipping soon.
- What will break if nothing changes.

Use time-based UX like:

- *Countdowns*: "Your compliance review is due in 14 days."
- *Forecasts*: "At this pace, your Q3 goal will fall short by 11%."
- *Decay alerts*: "This process slowed by 27% since last month."
- *Milestone nudges*: "You're two steps from completion—finish now to unlock X."
- *Recency scores*: "You haven't checked this report in 17 days. Here's what changed."

Give users a calendar-based reason to act. Not just features—deadlines. Product-led urgency isn't just about feature alerts—it's about shaping user behavior over time. The best SaaS companies treat their product like a coach: It doesn't just point out problems, it guides the next move. From onboarding sequences that front-load early wins to contextual prompts that teach while nudging, the product experience itself becomes a source of momentum. It tells users, "Here's why this matters—and here's what to do now."

HIGHLIGHT VALUE GAPS AND MISSED OPPORTUNITIES

Urgency isn't just about fixing what's broken. It's about seeing what's being missed. Features that work:

- "You're leaving money on the table" banners
- "Unlock 3× ROI" nudges tied to unused features
- "You've only automated 12% of your workflows" prompts
- "Competitors are seeing 2× faster outcomes with X" insights
- "This metric is underperforming for your industry" callouts

These don't criticize—they invite action. You're showing potential they can unlock—not blaming them for not having it yet.

BUILD DASHBOARDS THAT PRIORITIZE ACTION—NOT JUST DATA

Too many SaaS dashboards and reports are just rows of charts. But urgency requires clarity, contrast, and focus. A great dashboard answers:

- What's working?
- What's broken?
- What's trending down?
- What's at risk?
- What should I do next?

Use UI elements like:

- Color-coded priorities (red = urgent, yellow = watch, green = stable).
- Action cards ("Resolve this issue," "Assign a task," "Run analysis").
- Top three risks this week section.
- Next best action modules.
- "Fix this now" panels tied to specific metrics.

Dashboards should drive motion. Not just reflect it.

DESIGN EXECUTIVE VIEWS THAT DEMAND ATTENTION

Executives don't want to click around. They want:

- One screen.
- Summarized risk.
- Business impact.
- Time sensitivity.
- Recommendations.

Build exec dashboards that say: "Your risk is here. The opportunity is there. And if you don't act, this is what you'll lose."

Examples:

- "You're paying for 172 seats—only 64 are active. Savings potential: $32,400."
- "Onboarding delays are costing $41K/month in lost revenue."
- "Your churn risk has spiked 18%—here's the root cause."
- "These 3 workflows are slowing your top-performing team."

This isn't reporting. It's pressure—presented with precision.

NUDGE WITH PURPOSE—NOT JUST NOTIFICATIONS

Notifications often become noise. To create urgency:

- Keep alerts contextual (tied to the exact screen/task).
- Make them comparative ("You're 2× slower than peer teams").
- Add next steps ("Click here to fix it now").

- Be time-bound ("Act by Friday to stay compliant").
- Tie to goals ("This gap will cost 12% of target if unaddressed").

Avoid:

- "You haven't logged in" nags.
- "Check out this feature!" spam.
- Over-notifying for stable or trivial events.

Smart nudges guide behavior. Dumb nudges just annoy.

BUILD A MOMENTUM LOOP INSIDE THE TOOL

Urgency compounds when users see their progress—and their gaps. Inside the product:

- Show completed tasks: "You've remediated 82% of risks. Let's finish the last 18%."
- Track trend lines: "You've improved performance by 12% this month—keep it going."
- Compare to past: "You're resolving issues 3 days faster than last quarter."
- Set mini-challenges: "Hit 100% coverage by end of week."
- Enable sharing: "Send this win to your exec—2 clicks."

Let the product become a momentum engine—not just a tool.

REAL-WORLD EXAMPLE: SALES PRODUCTIVITY PLATFORM DRIVES DAILY ACTION

A sales productivity platform was seeing trouble signs. Reps were only logging in once or twice a week. Engagement was low. And as product usage declined, churn risk rose. The platform had all the right features—but it lacked urgency. So they flipped the model.

Instead of being a passive dashboard that waited to be opened, the product became a proactive, daily motivator. They redesigned the interface around micro-moments of action that reps couldn't ignore.

The updates included:

- *Live leaderboards*: "You're 3 calls behind your top peer—close the gap."
- *Action alerts*: "You haven't followed up on 6 hot leads. Take 5 minutes now."
- *AI nudges*: "This deal is stalling. Here's a high-converting CTA to try."
- *Quota progress meters*: "You're 76% to your weekly goal—finish strong."
- *Time sensitivity flags*: "This opportunity goes cold in 24 hours without action."

The change turned a static CRM into an urgency engine. The system began acting more like a coach than a tracker—identifying, prompting, and accelerating rep behavior every day.

The impact was immediate. Engagement rose by 40%, and reps started logging in daily. More importantly, usage led to outcomes: Pipeline velocity improved, conversions went up, and expansion conversations opened sooner because customers were seeing results.

The lesson? When your product prompts action—not just tracks it—urgency becomes part of your users' routine.

ALIGN PRODUCT URGENCY WITH GO-TO-MARKET URGENCY

Your product should echo the same urgency drivers your GTM motion uses.

If your sales deck says:

- "Most teams miss revenue due to broken onboarding."

Then your product should say:

- "Here's the bottleneck costing you 3 days per rep."

If your messaging says:

- "You're noncompliant with X regulation."

Then the product should say:

- "These 2 areas are exposed. Fix them by March 1."

When GTM and product align on the same fears, friction, and focus, urgency becomes continuous.

Action Checklist

- ☐ Build visual triggers inside the product that surface broken processes or risks.
- ☐ Use time-based elements like countdowns, forecasts, and milestone nudges.
- ☐ Highlight opportunity gaps and missed value in ways users can act on.
- ☐ Design dashboards to prioritize action—not just display data.
- ☐ Give executives high-level views that reveal cost, risk, and time-sensitive threats.
- ☐ Use intelligent nudges tied to behavior, benchmarks, and goals.
- ☐ Create momentum loops that show progress and encourage follow-through.
- ☐ Align product experience with GTM messaging to reinforce urgency at every touchpoint.

Chapter 31

USING PRICING AND PACKAGING TO DRIVE FASTER DECISIONS

Your pricing should do more than capture value. It should create urgency. But too often, pricing slows deals down. Why? Because it's:

- Too complicated.
- Too flexible.
- Too negotiable.
- Too disconnected from time.
- Too focused on what you *want to charge*—not what will make buyers *move fast*.

The best growth companies use pricing as a strategic lever—not just for revenue, but for velocity. This chapter is about how to structure your pricing and packaging to:

- Force prioritization.
- Limit procrastination.
- Incentivize urgency.
- Close more deals faster.

MAKE YOUR PRICING TIME SENSITIVE BY DEFAULT

Pricing should answer not just "How much?" but "Why now?" If your price is always the same—regardless of when a buyer signs—you remove one of your best urgency levers.

Fix that.

Ways to bake in time-based urgency:

- *Quarter-based incentives*: "Lock in Q2 pricing before rates increase next quarter."
- *Pilot credits that expire*: "You get $5K in onboarding credits if you start by May 15."
- *Price locks tied to implementation windows*: "We're holding your onboarding slot open until Friday."
- *Annual billing discounts with deadlines*: "This is our annual prepay rate—it resets at month end."
- *Price increase announcements*: "Our new pricing goes into effect June 1. You can still get the current rate."

Urgency works when there's *real consequence* tied to the calendar.

OFFER GOOD-BETTER-BEST (BUT DRIVE URGENCY TO THE MIDDLE)

Tiered pricing works best when:

- It makes the decision easier.
- It highlights the cost of compromise.
- It nudges buyers to move faster—to avoid missing the best value.

Here's how:

- Design your middle plan to be the clear value choice.
- Give the bottom plan obvious limitations (one user, missing features, etc.).
- Make the top plan aspirational (enterprise grade, scalable, white glove).
- Add urgency to the middle:
  - "15% off until [date]"
  - "Includes onboarding if signed by Friday"
  - "Locked-in rate for 2 years if purchased this month"

This creates a strong center of gravity—and a reason to buy now.

ANCHOR HIGH—THEN OFFER A SPEED-BASED PATH TO VALUE

The fastest way to build urgency in pricing? Make it feel like a deal. But only if they act fast.

Use value-based anchoring to:

- Show the cost of the problem you solve.
- Present the full scope of what your solution offers.
- Anchor with a higher plan or longer-term price.
- Then reduce scope only if they commit quickly.

Example: "Our platform typically runs $60K/year for your team size. But if we start with two modules and sign this week, we can roll out for $36K—and scale from there."

This isn't discounting. It's urgency-based scoping.

USE "UNLOCK PRICING" TO REWARD READINESS

Flip the script on traditional discounting. Instead of lowering price for indecision, lower it for action.

Try this:

- "You get our implementation rate reduced 30%—if we kick off this month."
- "Multiyear discounts are available—only if we finalize before the Q2 board meeting."
- "Full suite pricing is unlocked after the diagnostic. Let's run it this week."

This shifts the buyer's mindset from "How do I get a better price?" to "What do I need to do to unlock a better price?" That's urgency—with control and posture. One of the most underutilized urgency levers in pricing? Peer pressure. When buyers see others in their segment, industry, or buyer cohort already acting—at preferred rates or bundled packages—they feel the clock ticking. Use phrases like, "Five other companies in your space locked this in last week," or "We only offer this bundle to early movers in your category." Now pricing isn't just a math problem—it's a competitive motivator.

PRICE FOR SIMPLICITY, NOT COMPLEXITY

Complex pricing kills urgency.

Buyers stall when they're:

- Confused about value.
- Afraid of getting locked into the wrong tier.
- Unsure what's included.
- Unclear what the final cost will be.

Make your pricing:

- Clear (one-page summary, simple tiers).
- Transparent (visible on website or in shared docs).
- Predictable (no weird overage formulas).
- Framed around outcomes, not features.
- Scalable (so it's obvious how they grow).

The simpler your pricing, the faster the deal moves.

USE A "FAST START" OFFER FOR HESITANT BUYERS

Some buyers freeze not because of cost—but out of commitment fear.

Create urgency with a low-risk "fast start" offer:

- 60-day paid pilot with milestone-based expansion
- Small-team or single-module launch at a lower price
- "Land-and-expand" pricing that's time-boxed
- "Get value in 30 days or walk away" money-back clauses
- Credits that convert into full license later

Say:

"You don't have to commit to the full rollout now. Let's start small, prove it works, and move quickly from there." You reduce resistance. You increase urgency. You build trust.

MAKE EXPANSION MORE EXPENSIVE THAN ACTING NOW

Another urgency trick? Use future pricing friction to drive action today.

Examples:

- "Add-on pricing increases after initial contract is signed."
- "Additional seats are cheaper when bundled into the initial agreement."
- "Upgrades post-purchase require a new procurement process."
- "Custom integrations are included now—billed separately later."

You're not threatening. You're being real: "It's easier and cheaper to do this now—while we have momentum."

EQUIP SALES WITH URGENCY SCRIPTS AROUND PRICING

Even with a great pricing model, urgency dies if Sales can't communicate it.

Equip your reps with lines like:

- "This pricing is tied to our current launch program—it expires Friday."
- "We're offering preferred onboarding slots to teams who sign by quarter-end."
- "This incentive is limited to customers who participate in our early success pilot."
- "To lock this rate, we'd need to move this week—otherwise, we'll need to requote."

These aren't closing tricks. They're truthful time-based nudges. And they work.

REAL-WORLD EXAMPLE: DEVELOPER-TOOL COMPANY ACCELERATES SALES WITH URGENCY BUNDLING

A developer-tools company had a strong product, solid interest, and plenty of demos. But deals weren't closing fast enough. Buyers liked what they saw—but lacked a reason to move now. The sales cycle was dragging. So, instead of cutting prices, they reengineered how they packaged and positioned value.

They implemented a new pricing structure centered around urgency, not discounts:

- *Introduced a three-tier plan with clearly defined use cases*: It offered one for individuals, one for small dev teams, and one for enterprise buyers. Each plan mapped directly to the outcomes that buyer persona cared about most.
- *Debuted a "Launch Incentive" bundle every 45 days*: It included the core platform, a starter pack of most-used modules, and 60 days of premium onboarding support. But it came with a timer—if you didn't act, it expired.
- *Locked-in special pricing on add-on modules—but only if included in the initial contract*: Adding them later would cost significantly more, making early decisions feel smarter and safer.
- *Created a "Fast Track Pilot" option*: Buyers who signed by the end of the month got 20% off implementation services and a scoped success plan with clear 30-day outcomes.

The result? Sales cycle length dropped by 35%. Buyers began asking, "How can we secure this bundle now?" rather than "Let's evaluate this over the next few months." Discount haggling slowed because the structure itself carried built-in urgency. Expansion velocity doubled, as customers chose to go bigger up front to lock in pricing and avoid future costs.

This strategy proved a critical point: Urgency isn't always about slashing prices. It's about making the cost of waiting feel higher than the effort of acting now. And that power lies in how you structure the offer—not just what you charge.

Action Checklist

- ☐ Add time-based incentives to your pricing to reward fast action.
- ☐ Use good-better-best packages with urgency centered on the middle tier.
- ☐ Anchor high—and offer urgency-based scoping for early commitment.
- ☐ Reward readiness with unlockable pricing, not reactive discounts.
- ☐ Simplify your pricing structure to eliminate decision paralysis.
- ☐ Create fast-start offers that reduce commitment risk and speed up momentum.
- ☐ Make expansion or future features more expensive if not bundled now.
- ☐ Train your GTM team with urgency scripts and calendar-based pricing prompts.

Chapter 32

WINNING THE C-SUITE

How to Create Executive-Level Urgency

You've convinced the team. They love the demo. They see the need. They want to move. But the deal still doesn't close. Why? Because the C-suite hasn't bought in. And without executive urgency, deals stall, budgets freeze, and priorities shift. Here's the truth:

Champions don't close enterprise deals. Executives do.

If you want to accelerate pipeline, you need to create C-level urgency—the kind that breaks through noise, overcomes objections, and drives decisive action. This chapter is your guide to doing just that.

WHY EXECUTIVE URGENCY IS DIFFERENT

Executives care about:

- Strategic risk.
- Competitive advantage.
- Revenue growth.
- Market signals.
- Board expectations.
- Personal legacy.

They do not care about:

- Features.
- Integrations.
- Roadmaps.
- UX.
- Technical bells and whistles.

So if you're trying to win a CEO, CMO, CIO, or CFO using product demos and user pain . . . you'll lose. Instead, you must translate the urgency into their language—and their world.

TIE THE PROBLEM TO A STRATEGIC BUSINESS GOAL

Start by asking: "What initiative is this executive already committed to?"

Examples:

- Digital transformation
- Cost optimization
- Market expansion
- Operational efficiency
- Customer retention
- Risk mitigation
- Employee productivity
- AI or automation mandates

Then frame the problem as a threat to that goal: "You're investing in expansion, but your current onboarding process is delaying revenue by 3–4 weeks per hire. That's a hidden $2M drag on your plan." Now you're not just solving a problem. You're removing an obstacle to success.

QUANTIFY THE STRATEGIC COST OF INACTION

Executives don't just need to know the benefit—they need to know the risk of delay.

Don't say:

"Our platform streamlines operations."

Say:

"Every month you delay rollout, you lose $180K in operational waste. That's $2.1M annually—from processes you've already outgrown."

Better yet:

- *Show benchmarks*: "Top-quartile firms in your space are operating 22% leaner in this area."
- *Show competitive signals*: "Your top two competitors have invested in this shift already—you're now 6–12 months behind."
- *Show compounding risk*: "The risk gap grows monthly—and you won't see the fallout until Q3."

Executives act when *the cost of inaction becomes visible, measurable, and growing.*

FRAME THE DECISION AROUND MARKET TIMING

Executives understand cycles—fiscal years, budgets, board reporting, earnings calls, planning seasons. Create urgency by tying action to regular events:

- "We're in budget finalization—this gets you in Q2 planning."
- "Board reporting is next month—we'll deliver metrics you can share."
- "Our program aligns with your AI initiative—this is the quarter to show progress."

- “Your competitors are already piloting—let’s keep you ahead of the pack.”
- “There’s a 90-day window before customer feedback gets worse. You don’t want to explain that uptick in churn.”

Executives don’t just ask, “Is this worth doing?” They ask: “Is this the right time?” Make the answer obvious. Executives are also deeply influenced by what their peers are doing—especially when those peers are solving the same problems faster. Name-drop competitors, reference recent moves in the market, or highlight strategic pivots from industry leaders. Say things like: “Your peers at [Company X] are already reporting board-level impact from this shift,” or “Two of your top competitors are now operationalizing this capability.” When urgency is framed as falling behind—not just missing opportunity—it rises to the top of the executive agenda.

SPEAK TO POWER, NOT PROCESS

Executives want insight. They want clarity. They want to feel in control. So, speak in terms of:

- Revenue risk.
- Brand protection.
- Investor pressure.
- People performance.
- Executive credibility.
- Market perception.

Avoid:

- “Let me walk you through our platform.”
- “Here’s how the automation works.”
- “We can integrate with your CRM in 3 steps.”

Instead:

"You've invested in growth. We're showing where hidden operational drag is slowing your team—and how we remove it this quarter."

Your tone should match theirs:

- Crisp
- Strategic
- Future focused
- No fluff
- All signal, no noise

USE A STRATEGIC BRIEF, NOT A SALES DECK

When speaking to execs, use a one-page Strategic Brief, not a sales deck. It should include:

- Executive Summary (one- or two-sentence problem framing).
- Business Impact (quantified pain or upside).
- Risk of Delay (what happens if they wait).
- Strategic Alignment (which initiative this supports).
- Recommended Action (clear CTA with timeline).

One page. Visually clean. Boardroom ready. Hand it to your champion and say: "If you want to drive this forward, here's the page your execs need." You're not selling. You're enabling internal urgency at the top.

POSITION YOURSELF AS A STRATEGIC PARTNER—NOT A VENDOR

Executives don't buy tools. They invest in strategic partnerships. To do that:

- Bring data they don't have.
- Show trends they're underestimating.
- Reveal risks they can't see.
- Connect your solution to outcomes they already care about.
- Be brief, but bold.

Language to use:

"You've got a bold vision. We're here to remove friction from that execution—fast."

"We're seeing similar companies move now to avoid Q3 exposure."

"Our customers use this data in board meetings to justify transformation budgets."

They should walk away thinking: "This isn't software. This is fuel for what we're already doing."

ASK EXEC-ONLY QUESTIONS THAT MAKE THEM THINK

Executives don't want demos. They want to be challenged.

Ask:

- "What's the biggest internal risk to hitting your goals this year?"
- "Where do you feel behind your competitors?"
- "What data is missing from your board conversations?"
- "Which initiative is most at risk of slipping this quarter?"
- "If you had to cut tools—what would make yours unkillable?"

These questions spark real urgency—not artificial FOMO. And they earn you trust.

REAL-WORLD EXAMPLE: FINTECH SAAS WINS THE CFO FAST

A fintech SaaS company had strong momentum with mid-market operations teams. Their champions loved the platform, demos were engaging, and use cases were clear. But there was a bottleneck—CFOs. Despite internal buy-in, deals kept getting delayed once they hit Finance. The issue wasn't interest—it was inertia at the executive level.

So they rewrote their approach. Instead of continuing to sell features or operational benefits, they pivoted to selling to the CFO's priorities: cash flow, efficiency, and financial optics.

They built a five-part CFO acceleration play:

- *A "Cost of Delay" brief* that reframed waiting as a financial loss. It clearly quantified how operational drag—delayed vendor payments, slow reconciliations, and cash forecasting inaccuracies—was costing the business every month.
- *A competitive benchmark* that named a rival company who implemented the same system six months earlier—and had just posted improved working capital and margin efficiency in their earnings call. It turned delay into a reputational risk.
- *A personalized calculator* that showed exactly how much money the company was leaving on the table: "Based on your numbers, that's $312,000 in avoidable annual loss—every month you wait, it compounds."
- *A 60-day ROI roadmap* that laid out what Finance could expect in the first two months—faster closes, fewer manual entries, and improved visibility for reporting. It wasn't aspirational. It was pragmatic.
- *A financial justification template* the champion could use to make the case internally, including ROI

projections, implementation cost breakdowns, and references from finance leaders at peer companies.

The result? CFOs stopped stalling. They started asking questions. They invited finance leaders into the conversation earlier. Deals accelerated. Champions were no longer stuck explaining—they had air cover.

Most importantly, the seller wasn't just pitching a better way to run ops. They were showing CFOs how to be heroes—fiscally responsible, proactive, and ahead of the curve.

They weren't just selling software. They were manufacturing executive momentum.

Action Checklist

- ☐ Map your solution to the buyer's strategic initiatives.
- ☐ Quantify the cost of inaction in terms that matter to the C-suite.
- ☐ Tie urgency to market timing, planning cycles, and competitive shifts.
- ☐ Eliminate jargon—speak in strategy, risk, ROI, and impact.
- ☐ Create a one-page Strategic Brief for champions to use with execs.
- ☐ Position yourself as a growth partner—not a technical tool.
- ☐ Ask thought-provoking, executive-only questions to trigger reflection.
- ☐ Elevate the urgency conversation to where real decisions are made.

Chapter 33

MULTIPLY URGENCY THROUGH SELLERS AND PARTNERS

If urgency is the force that drives action, then your greatest accelerators are the people on the front lines—your sales reps and channel partners.

But here's the hard truth: Most sellers aren't naturally wired to create urgency. They're trained to explain value. They're taught to differentiate. But few know how to make the status quo feel uncomfortable—and that's the missing piece.

The good news? Urgency can be engineered. Not just in marketing. Not just through campaigns. But at the human-to-human level, where deals are made or lost. This chapter shows you how to equip your reps and partners to do just that.

STEP 1: TRAIN SALES REPS TO LEAD WITH CONSEQUENCES, NOT CAPABILITIES

Too often, salespeople open with what the product does.

But urgency is created when you start with what happens if the customer does nothing.

Instead of:

"Let me show you what we can do."

Teach your reps to start with:

"Let's talk about what's likely to happen if nothing changes."

Help them shift from selling features to framing consequences. That's where urgency lives.

STEP 2: GIVE REPS THE TOOLS TO EXPOSE THE HIDDEN PAIN

Great sellers don't invent pain. They expose what already exists—and help the buyer see it clearly for the first time.

Arm your team with:

- Discovery questions that surface problems buyers haven't quantified.
- Free tools or assessments that reveal measurable gaps.
- Customer stories that show the real-world cost of waiting.

When the buyer says, "That's exactly what we're dealing with," you've done your job.

STEP 3: ROLEPLAY URGENCY, NOT OBJECTION HANDLING

Most sales training spends hours on objection handling—but devotes little time to rehearsing urgency conversations.

Shift your sales enablement focus to:

- Practicing how to guide a buyer from "It's not a priority" to "We can't afford to wait."

- Building urgency into follow-ups: "Has the risk changed—or is it still as real as last week?"
- Helping reps identify and deepen urgency signals, not just qualification criteria.

Urgency isn't a closing tactic. It's a conversation style—one that must be trained.

STEP 4: TURN CHANNEL PARTNERS INTO URGENCY AMPLIFIERS

Most channel partners don't wake up thinking about your product. They wake up thinking about how to hit their own numbers.

If you want them to drive urgency, give them tools that:

- Make problems visible fast (scans, reports, diagnostics).
- Make urgency their advantage in a deal ("Use this free tool to prove the risk to your prospect").
- Make their follow-up consultative, not transactional.

Train partners to ask questions like:

"What grade did your customer get on the assessment?"

"Where did they fall short—and how does that affect their business today?"

When partners feel like they're helping, not just selling, they become invested.

STEP 5: GIVE REPS AND PARTNERS AN URGENCY PLAYBOOK

Build a simple, repeatable playbook for creating urgency. Include:

- Common "comfort zone" beliefs prospects hold (e.g., "We're already secure").
- The cost of those beliefs (e.g., "Here's what's actually happening in environments like yours").
- Proof tools (data, reports, peer comparisons).
- Emotional levers (personal risk, missed goals, exposure).
- Call-to-action language that invites, not pushes.

The playbook should be used in onboarding, coaching, and quarterly business reviews. It's not a one-and-done document—it's part of your growth culture.

Urgency doesn't scale on its own. It must be taught. Modeled. Reinforced. The companies that grow fast don't just create urgency through marketing. They multiply it through people. And those who sell with urgency don't just close more deals—they change the way their buyers think.

STEP 6: SET AND ENFORCE SLAS FOR SPEED AND FOLLOW-THROUGH

Urgency doesn't stick if there's no follow-through. One of the biggest killers of momentum is silence after signal—when a lead fills out a form, a buyer shows interest, or a partner surfaces an opportunity . . . and no one moves fast enough.

That's why SLAs aren't optional. They're your enforcement mechanism for urgency.

Great GTM organizations set SLAs that define:

- How fast reps must follow up on inbound leads (e.g., within 15 minutes).
- How long it should take to convert discovery to proposal.
- What timelines partners should follow when handing off deals.
- How quickly enablement materials or technical answers are expected in shared deals.

And most importantly—they track compliance and make it visible.

Why it matters:

- Buyers respond to responsiveness. Every hour you wait, interest decays.
- Partners feel supported (or forgotten) based on how quickly you react.
- Managers can diagnose where urgency breaks down—and fix it in real time.

SLAs aren't bureaucracy. They're commitment—to speed, to action, and to winning together.

Action Checklist

- ☐ Train reps to lead with cost of inaction, not capabilities.
- ☐ Equip sellers with free tools or assessments that reveal measurable risk.
- ☐ Embed urgency into roleplay, coaching, and onboarding.
- ☐ Enable partners with tools that help them reveal the problem, not just sell the product.
- ☐ Create a repeatable urgency playbook and make it core to your enablement programs—and include SLAs for sales rep follow-up.
- ☐ Reinforce urgency with storytelling, benchmarks, and buyer self-assessments.
- ☐ Track urgency-driven selling behaviors in your pipeline reviews and quarterly business reviews (QBRs).

Chapter 34

WINNING WEBSITE TRAFFIC IN THE AI ERA—BEFORE IT'S TOO LATE

Website traffic is collapsing for many companies—and it's not by accident. CMOs and CROs who bet on generic, AI-generated content as their growth engine are already paying the price: declining traffic, fewer leads, shrinking pipelines, and missed revenue goals. The shift is happening fast—AI engines reward depth, authority, and originality, not copycat content. If you're not urgently adapting your strategy to create the kind of content AI trusts and cites, you will lose visibility to competitors who are. The playbook has changed. This chapter lays out what you must do now to reverse the decline and grow traffic when everyone else is losing it.

WHY AI-GENERATED CONTENT FAILS TO DRIVE REFERRALS

When it comes to referral traffic from generative AI engines like ChatGPT, Perplexity, or Gemini, the algorithms reward uniqueness, depth, and credibility. AI-generated content fails on all three counts:

- *It's generic*: Such content is often repackaged from what's already online, with little differentiation.
- *It lacks authority*: Buyers and AI alike look for credibility rooted in expertise.
- *It doesn't build trust signals*: AI models and search engines elevate content with backlinks, citations, and expert commentary—things AI-only content rarely achieves.
- *It's undifferentiated noise*: As more companies flood the market with AI blogs, visibility diminishes rather than grows.

If your strategy is "AI writes blogs, AI recommends blogs, AI drives traffic," you've already lost.

WHAT ACTUALLY WINS: HUMAN-EXPERT-LED CONTENT

The only proven way to increase referrals from AI engines and grow organic traffic while others see declines is to publish expert-driven, unique, actionable content. This is the type of content AI trusts and cites. Here's what works:

- *Subject-Matter Expert Insights*: Elevate internal experts by capturing their real-world lessons and unique perspectives.
- *Gartner-Style Comparisons*: Provide structured head-to-head evaluations and buyer's guides.
- *Deep "How To" White Papers*: Deliver step-by-step playbooks practitioners can apply immediately.

- *Unique Research & Benchmarks*: Share proprietary data, surveys, and industry benchmarks.
- *Case Studies with Real Numbers*: Publish proof points that competitors and AI cannot replicate.

THE FORMULA TO GROW WEBSITE TRAFFIC (AND REVENUE)

The companies that will dominate in the AI referral era aren't the ones publishing the most AI-written blogs. They're the ones producing analyst-style depth infused with real human expertise. The formula is simple:

- AI-only content ≠ visibility. It gets ignored.
- SME + data-driven content = trust. This kind of content will be cited by AI, analysts, and customers.
- Unique thought leadership = pipeline. Appearing in AI responses becomes a direct revenue accelerator.

The key to winning more referrals from AI is to stop depending on it as the creator and instead feed it authoritative, differentiated content. Companies that embrace this shift will see traffic, leads, and revenue grow while competitors continue to decline.

Action Checklist

- ☐ Audit your current content: Separate AI-generic from SME-led.
- ☐ Establish weekly SME-driven content publishing.
- ☐ Invest in quarterly benchmarks, reports, and comparisons to be the "source of truth."
- ☐ Prioritize backlinks through data, research, and case studies.
- ☐ Track referral traffic not just from search, but from generative AI sources.

Chapter 35

CREATING URGENCY ON YOUR MARKETING TEAM

Your marketing team doesn't just shape urgency externally—it must live it internally.

If your marketers aren't moving fast, pushing hard, and acting with a clear clock ticking in their heads, your pipeline suffers. And here's the truth: Too many marketing teams are busy, but not urgent. They're creating, publishing, planning—but not producing momentum. The energy is real, but the velocity is missing.

Urgency on your marketing team doesn't mean panic. It means precision. It means clarity. It means knowing what moves the needle and focusing relentlessly on that. This chapter is about how to build a marketing team that thinks and operates with urgency—so that urgency shows up in your funnel.

SET NONNEGOTIABLE, MEASURABLE GOALS TIED TO YOUR PIPELINE

Nothing creates urgency like accountability. If your marketing team isn't being held to pipeline and revenue goals—clearly, directly, and publicly—they won't feel the same heat as Sales.

Make the goal visible. Make it time-bound. Make it tied to outcomes, not outputs.

Not "How many blog posts?" but "How many opportunities?"

Not "Did we launch the campaign?" but "Did it convert?"

KILL THE COMFORT OF VANITY METRICS

Open rates don't pay the bills. Neither do likes, shares, or webinar registrants who never engage again.

Urgent marketing teams track:

- Visitor-to-lead conversion
- Marketing-qualified leads (MQL) to SQL conversion
- Pipeline sourced and influenced
- Sales velocity impact

When your KPIs get sharper, so does your pace.

OPERATE IN SPRINTS, NOT SEASONS

Urgency hates bureaucracy. It thrives in focused, fast cycles.

Move from annual campaign planning to agile marketing sprints:

- Every two weeks, review goals, measure what worked, kill what didn't, and double down on what did.
- Assign ownership for every priority.
- Make performance visible across sales, product, and leadership.

Speed isn't a side effect. It's a decision.

FEATURE THE VOICES OF SALES AND CUSTOMERS IN MEETINGS

Marketers lose urgency when they lose contact with reality.

Embed live sales calls, post-deal win/loss feedback, or top rep insights into every team meeting. Make sure the team hears what real buyers are saying—now. Urgency spikes when marketers know the deal is on the line.

PRIORITIZE RUTHLESSLY—AND SAY NO OFTEN

Most marketing teams are overwhelmed because they're doing too much.

Urgent teams ask:

- What moves pipeline in the next 30 days?
- What will get used by Sales?
- What are we creating that no one asked for?

They don't chase everything. They chase what accelerates.

CELEBRATE WINS THAT CREATE MOVEMENT, NOT JUST WORK

Reward the team for outcomes, not activity.

Recognize the marketer who delivered pipeline, not just the one who hit "publish." Celebrate the landing page that converted, not just the brand refresh that got compliments. Urgency becomes culture when the reward system reinforces it.

PUT DEADLINES IN DAYS, NOT MONTHS

Parkinson's Law says work expands to fill the time available. So, make less time available.

Urgency dies when teams wait weeks for feedback, approvals, or collaboration. Set deadlines in days. Review daily. Ship weekly. Fast teams don't ask, "Can we do it?" They ask, "How do we get it live this week?"

MODEL IT FROM THE TOP

If marketing leaders don't show urgency, no one will.

Move fast. Give feedback immediately. Kill low-impact work openly. Reprioritize often. Show your team that you're not here to be busy—you're here to make buyers move. You can't expect your prospects to feel urgency if your marketers don't.

Urgency is contagious. When it lives inside your team—in their mindset, metrics, and habits—it shows up in your market. And that's when things start to move.

Action Checklist

- ☐ Set clear, public pipeline goals tied to marketing output.
- ☐ Kill vanity metrics in favor of conversion and pipeline KPIs.
- ☐ Run weekly or biweekly marketing sprints.
- ☐ Feed sales calls and buyer feedback into team meetings.
- ☐ Prioritize high-velocity impact over "nice-to-have" tasks.
- ☐ Celebrate speed, learning, and pipeline contribution.
- ☐ Enforce short, tight deadlines and rapid iteration.
- ☐ Model urgency from marketing leadership every day.

Chapter 36

TURNING RENEWALS INTO REVENUE EVENTS

Most companies treat renewals like administrative tasks. Auto-reminders. Invoice cycles. Contract PDFs. But great companies treat renewals as revenue events—a strategic opportunity to:

- Reignite urgency.
- Expand usage.
- Reinforce executive commitment.
- Capture more value.
- Launch the next phase of the journey.

Renewals aren't about keeping what you have. They're about unlocking what's next. This chapter is about how to turn your renewal motion into a revenue engine—by building urgency, not just retention.

WHY RENEWALS ARE RIPE FOR URGENCY

By the time a renewal approaches, three things are typically true:

1. Your buyer has more experience with your product.
2. Internal priorities have shifted—fast.
3. Other vendors are circling.

If you treat this as a passive moment—"Let's get the paperwork done"—you miss the chance to:

- Reopen the conversation at a higher level.
- Quantify impact and justify expansion.
- Expose new risks or gaps.
- Prevent silent churn (a.k.a. renewals without engagement).
- Upgrade your seat at the strategic table.

A renewal is your second chance to spark urgency—and do it better than you did the first time.

Step 1: Start the Renewal Process 60–90 Days Early—as a Business Review

Don't start with procurement. Start with value. Kick off with a 60- to 90-day strategic business review. Not a QBR. Not a usage report.

A business review should include:

- *Outcome summary*: "Here's what we helped you achieve."
- *Missed opportunities*: "Here's what you could've done—but didn't."
- *Risk status*: "Here's where exposure still exists."
- *Benchmarking*: "Here's how you compare to peers."
- *Strategic alignment*: "Here's how we tie into your next initiatives."

Then, pivot to: "Here's what we recommend for the next 12 months—and why now matters." Make the review forward facing—not just retrospective.

Step 2: Create a Renewal Scorecard—and Let the Buyer Self-Diagnose

Instead of defending your value, let them realize it. Use a simple scorecard that shows:

- Feature adoption.
- Business impact (e.g., time saved, dollars protected, risk reduced).
- Cross-team usage.
- Support utilization.
- Strategic alignment.
- Executive engagement.
- Expansion potential.

Example:

Area	Status
Workflow Automation	✓ Fully adopted
Compliance Alerts	✗ Not activated
Integration with CRM	⚠ Partial
Department Rollout	✗ 1 of 4 completed
Monthly Reports	✓ Delivered

Let them see the gaps. Then say: "We've achieved a lot. But you've only tapped into 42% of the platform's potential. Let's change that this year." Urgency comes from *what's still possible.*

Step 3: Introduce a New Threat—or a New Opportunity

Renewals often lose momentum because the original pain has faded. Fix that by introducing something new:

- A compliance change
- A competitive signal
- A market trend
- A business initiative shift

- A leadership change
- A usage risk ("You're underutilizing a key feature—and it's putting you behind.")

Examples:

"AI compliance guidelines were just updated. You're out of step with two of the five new frameworks."

"Your top competitor just adopted workflow automation—cutting their turnaround time by 28%."

Even if the original pain is solved, new urgency creates new momentum.

Step 4: Bundle Expansion into the Renewal Window

Don't just fight for the same contract. Use the renewal moment to:

- Add new teams or users.
- Activate unused modules.
- Upgrade support or services.
- Expand regions.
- Launch integrations.
- Move to a higher-value plan.

Create expansion bundles like:

- "Renew + expand by [date] to lock in multiyear pricing."
- "Free onboarding for the new module if included now."
- "Upgrade to enterprise support for 50% off—renewal only."
- "Convert your success into a case study—and unlock executive training."

You're not just preserving value. You're compounding it.

Step 5: Reengage the Executive Sponsor

By renewal time, execs often disengage. Reignite that thread by:

- Creating a one-page ROI report (outcomes, metrics, benchmarks).
- Sending a personalized video or email from your CEO.
- Framing the renewal as a strategic reset.
- Positioning expansion as a C-level win tied to key initiatives.

Say: "You made the bet last year. It paid off. Now let's scale it—in a way that drives board-level results."

Executives don't want to revisit decisions. They want to feel like the next chapter matters. Renewals are also your best chance to activate advocacy. Right after securing the renewal—especially if it includes an upgrade—ask the champion or executive to share their success. This might be a quick quote, a LinkedIn comment, or a case study kickoff. Don't wait for "perfect results"—urgency fades fast. If you wait, you miss the window when energy, gratitude, and visibility are at their peak.

Step 6: Create a Deadline with a Clear Reason

Don't let renewals float into oblivion. Create urgency with a meaningful deadline.

Examples:

- "We can secure this pricing if signed by month end."
- "This expansion bundle expires June 15."
- "New implementation resources are available now—but we're booking fast."
- "Your audit window opens in Q3—we need to be live by then."
- "Your CFO wants this off the books before the next cycle."

Urgency without reason feels pushy. Urgency with context feels responsible.

Step 7: Incentivize Speed Without Discounting the Core

Resist discounting the base renewal. Instead:

- Offer incentives tied to expansion.
- Tie benefits to early commitment.
- Add value instead of subtracting cost.

Examples:

- "Renew and expand by June 1 → 3 months of premium support free."
- "Prepay annual plan → executive dashboard module included."
- "Sign by May 15 → onboarding for new region included at no cost."
- "Add 2 new teams → get a 30-day pilot success sprint with our solutions team."

This creates *good pressure*—while preserving long-term pricing integrity.

REAL-WORLD EXAMPLE: AI VENDOR TURNS RENEWAL INTO A BOARDROOM MOMENT

An AI-powered analytics platform had a $180K annual recurring revenue (ARR) customer approaching renewal. Historically, their process was simple: Send the invoice, offer a quick check-in, and hope for a signature. But this time, they saw an opportunity—not just to retain the customer, but to reignite urgency and expand the relationship.

Instead of sending a generic renewal reminder, they engineered a boardroom-level play:

- *Renewal Readiness Scorecard*: They delivered a report card that highlighted only 60% feature adoption. Not as a failure—but as untapped upside. It included a visual showing which high-impact features hadn't been used yet and how that was limiting performance across key business lines.
- *C-Suite Impact Report*: They reframed the value delivered at the executive level: "Your team improved strategic decision-making cycle time by 14%." This wasn't usage. This was outcome—language the COO, CFO, and board would care about.
- *Competitive Benchmark*: They showed that peer

organizations in the same sector were automating 2× more workflows using similar tooling. This wasn't just a pat on the back—it was a subtle wake-up call. "You're ahead—but you could fall behind."

- *Emerging Risk Alert*: They uncovered a new issue: "Data drift is now impacting three production models—these were stable last year." This wasn't a scare tactic. It was a proactive threat disclosure—and a reason to act before the renewal even came due.
- *Strategic Upsell Offer*: They bundled an offer to expand usage: "Add two AI optimization modules and extend to a multiyear term—get 20% cost efficiency and dedicated success engineering." This wasn't a sales pitch. It was a scale plan.
- *Executive-Level Nudge*: Last, the vendor's chief revenue officer sent a personalized note to the customer's COO: "Your data team has laid the foundation. Now's the time to take full advantage. Here's how we'll partner with you to make it happen."

The result?

- The customer didn't just renew—they renewed early.
- They signed a larger contract with a 50% increase in footprint.
- They committed to two new AI modules.
- They secured C-suite sponsorship to drive adoption even deeper.

They didn't just protect a deal. They reset the narrative.

By making the renewal about progress, risk, and opportunity—not maintenance—the vendor turned a routine commercial event into a strategic inflection point. They didn't renew a contract. They renewed urgency.

Action Checklist

- ☐ Begin renewal motion 60–90 days in advance with a forward-looking business review.
- ☐ Use a visual scorecard to highlight gaps in usage, impact, or adoption.
- ☐ Introduce a new risk, trend, or opportunity to spark fresh urgency.
- ☐ Bundle expansion into the renewal to create a next-chapter plan.
- ☐ Reengage the executive sponsor with data, outcomes, and vision.
- ☐ Set a firm renewal deadline tied to business, fiscal, or operational context.
- ☐ Offer incentives tied to expansion or early action—not discounts on base.
- ☐ Treat the renewal as a strategic moment—not just a subscription event.

Chapter 37

THE 90-DAY URGENCY SPRINT

Sometimes, urgency isn't just something you create in messaging. Sometimes, it needs to become a movement, across:

- Sales.
- Marketing.
- Customer success.
- Product.
- Leadership.

You don't need a full rebrand. You don't need months of workshops. You just need a focused 90-day sprint where everyone rallies around one goal: *Make the market move. Now.* This chapter is a step-by-step framework to inject urgency into your GTM engine—quickly, collaboratively, and with measurable impact.

WHY A SPRINT WORKS BETTER THAN A CAMPAIGN

Most urgency plays get buried inside:

- Quarterly content calendars.
- Product marketing updates.
- CRM automation.
- New feature releases.

They lose momentum. They get deprioritized. They spread too thin. But a sprint has:

- A defined window.
- Clear owners.
- Shared language.
- Aligned metrics.
- Executive attention.

It's not "business as usual." It's focused, high-impact activity designed to change behavior in a short window.

Step 1: Pick a Core Problem to Ignite the Sprint

The first step is to anchor the sprint in a specific, urgent problem that resonates with your buyers. Not a vague theme like "AI-powered workflows." Instead, say:

- "Revenue teams are leaking $X per month due to misrouted leads."
- "Mid-market CISOs are 6–12 months behind new compliance mandates."
- "IT teams are overwhelmed by SaaS bloat—and exposed to shadow risk."

Choose one. Make it:

- Quantifiable.
- Painful.
- Overlooked or underestimated.
- Easy to visualize.
- Aligned with your product's value.

This becomes the *North Star of the sprint.*

Step 2: Create a "Sprint Manifesto" for Internal Teams

Write a one-page internal doc that says:

- What we're solving.
- Why now.
- Who we're targeting.
- What we'll deliver.
- What success looks like.

Share it across:

- Sales.
- Marketing.
- Product.
- Success.
- Executive leadership.

Your message: "For the next 90 days, we're aligning around one urgent story—and we're going to flood the market with it."

Step 3: Launch with a Visible Moment

Start with an event that signals the sprint has begun.

Options:

- A LinkedIn Live or webinar titled: "The Hidden Risk That's Costing You $X a Month"
- A free diagnostic or benchmark tool
- A report drop with analyst commentary
- A CEO email blast that starts with: "There's something you need to see"

Make it:

- Emotional.
- Visual.
- Shareable.
- Quantifiable.
- Deadline driven.

This is your match strike. If you want to win executive attention during the sprint, dedicate one moment specifically for them. That could be a custom C-level webinar, a private ROI insight brief, or an executive-only diagnostic summary. These aren't just invites—they're strategic signals that say, "This sprint isn't just noise. It's boardroom relevant." Without executive traction, urgency stays tactical.

Step 4: Arm Sales with Urgency Assets

Don't just tell reps to "push harder." Give them the tools.

Examples:

- Talk tracks tied to the threat
- A "Cost of Delay" calculator
- Competitive slides showing market shift
- One-pager for exec buyers
- Objection handling for "let's wait" stalls
- ROI benchmarks from early adopters
- Email copy prewritten for reactivation

Let every rep lead with the same urgency narrative—reinforced with data, visuals, and peer examples.

Step 5: Make Your Website Urgency-Centric

Your homepage and landing pages should reflect the sprint. Tactics:

- New above-the-fold headline tied to the threat
- CTA to run the diagnostic or take the benchmark
- Visuals that show cost, risk, and time-to-fix

- Real-world examples and mini case studies
- Deadline-based banners ("Get your risk score by June 1")

This is not "evergreen." This is campaign-specific design, built to convert urgency into action.

Step 6: Run Weekly Progress Rituals

The sprint must be *managed like a mission.* Every week:

- Review campaign performance.
- Share win stories across teams.
- Highlight blockers and remove friction.
- Track urgency signals (lead response time, time-to-meeting, demo-to-decision lag).
- Celebrate urgency-based closes or reactivations.

Make it:

- Visible.
- Fast.
- Cross-functional.

You're not just reviewing pipeline. You're reinforcing a culture of velocity.

Step 7: Stack the Sprint with "Trigger Moments"

Don't rely on one splashy launch. Create waves across the 90 days.

Examples:

- Week 1: Risk scan or benchmark tool
- Week 2: Webinar or analyst briefing
- Week 3: Email campaign with urgency checklist
- Week 4: SDR blitz with cost-of-delay message
- Week 6: LinkedIn influencer post + comments
- Week 7: ROI proof from new customer

- Week 9: "Last chance" email + pricing deadline
- Week 12: Board-level deck template download

Every few weeks, ask, "What moment are we creating now?" Keep the market on edge. Keep the urgency alive.

Step 8: End with a Deadline and a Roll-Up

Every sprint needs a clear finish line.

Examples:

- "Q2 pricing bundle expires June 30."
- "Free onboarding ends this month."
- "Risk diagnostic closes after July 15."

Then:

- Roll up results.
- Publish a customer success story.
- Create a Sprint Retrospective (what worked, what to repeat, what to expand).
- Launch a second sprint, or fold urgency tactics into evergreen GTM.

Don't let urgency evaporate. *Evolve it.*

REAL-WORLD EXAMPLE: CYBERSECURITY FIRM RUNS A SPRINT—AND DOUBLES PIPELINE

A midstage cybersecurity company found its pipeline stagnating. Despite strong customer outcomes, the market was complacent. Their message—centered around MFA—wasn't cutting through. So, they launched a 90-day urgency sprint with a bold new narrative: "The Unseen Breach Risk: Why Your MFA Isn't Enough."

The campaign was a coordinated blitz, designed to activate fear, insight, and immediacy:

- *Risk Visualization Tool*: They launched a three-minute "exposure scan" that analyzed a prospect's identity and access environment, then flagged critical MFA blind spots—like inactive users with lingering admin privileges or shared credentials that bypassed MFA altogether.
- *CISO-Led Kickoff Webinar*: The campaign began with a live event featuring a well-known CISO who shared real-world breach scenarios where MFA failed—and how attackers were exploiting gaps no one was watching. Attendance tripled expectations.
- *SDR Activation Kit*: SDRs were armed with personalized "Breach Exposure Briefs"—lightweight PDF reports that showed prospects where they were most vulnerable, even if they *thought* MFA had them covered. These reports became their highest-performing follow-up asset in 12 months.
- *Homepage Takeover*: The company's website was reskinned to focus entirely on "exposed surface area." An animated visualization showed how MFA protections created a false sense of security—while lateral access pathways remained wide open.
- *Sales Standups + Leaderboards*: Every week, the sales team met to review sprint metrics—calls made, briefs delivered, pipeline created—with public leaderboards to foster friendly competition and urgency inside the team.

- *"Before July 1" Pricing Anchor*: They set a hard deadline for new clients to lock in implementation support and legacy pricing before a new compliance-driven tier launched. This wasn't a gimmick—it was framed as "You'll want to be protected before the Q3 breach spike, and this is the easiest way to do it."

THE RESULTS

In just 90 days:

- Pipeline doubled.
- Sales cycle shortened by 27%.
- Twenty-two stale opportunities reactivated.
- Three C-level expansion calls booked from existing customers near renewal.

But more than metrics—the sprint changed market behavior. Prospects who once said, "We're covered" started asking, "Can we get scanned this week?" They felt the threat. Fast. And everywhere.

Why it worked: Because they didn't run a campaign. They staged a sprint. They didn't just tell the market why they were different. They made the market feel why now mattered.

Action Checklist

- ☐ Choose one urgent, quantifiable problem to anchor the sprint.
- ☐ Write and share a one-page Sprint Manifesto across GTM teams.
- ☐ Launch with a bold, visual, public activation moment.
- ☐ Equip Sales with data-driven urgency talk tracks, tools, and content.
- ☐ Redesign website CTAs and visuals to reflect the sprint narrative.
- ☐ Run weekly check-ins to track urgency behaviors and share wins.
- ☐ Stack the sprint with new "trigger moments" every few weeks.
- ☐ End with a clear deadline—and package results for momentum.

Chapter 38

MEASURING THE IMPACT OF URGENCY

Creating urgency is a powerful growth lever. But if you can't measure it, you can't prove it. And if you can't prove it, urgency becomes just another marketing idea—not a business driver. The goal of this chapter is simple: to show you how to measure urgency so clearly, your CEO asks why you didn't do it sooner.

Urgency isn't fluff. It's trackable. It's scalable. It's a repeatable motion with measurable ROI. Here's how to prove it.

WHAT "URGENCY IMPACT" REALLY MEANS

Urgency is not a vanity metric. It's not:

- "More clicks."
- "Higher open rates."
- "More engagement."

Those may be signs of interest—but interest is not action.
Urgency drives:

- Faster decisions.
- Bigger deals.
- Higher close rates.
- Shorter sales cycles.
- More meeting bookings.
- More budget unlocked.
- Stronger executive involvement.
- Expansion and renewal acceleration.

Your measurement plan must track the things *urgency actually moves.*

SET A CLEAR BASELINE

Before you can prove impact, you need to know: "What does our current velocity and conversion look like?" Key baseline metrics:

- Lead-to-meeting time
- Demo-to-decision time
- Average sales cycle by segment
- Deals stalled >30 days
- MQLs to SQL conversion
- Pipeline influenced by urgency campaigns
- Average deal size
- Stakeholder count per deal
- Time-to-value after onboarding

Capture this before you run urgency plays. Then compare after. That delta is your proof.

TRACK CAMPAIGN-LEVEL URGENCY PERFORMANCE

Any campaign designed to spark urgency should be measured by:

- *Speed*: How fast do buyers engage or respond?
- *Depth*: How far into the funnel do they go?
- *Decision momentum*: Are they acting faster than the control group?

Example metrics:

- Time from click → booking
- Time from scan/diagnostic → qualified conversation
- Average number of stakeholders engaged
- % of opportunities touching urgency content (like a cost calculator or benchmark)
- Win rates of urgency-influenced deals vs. standard deals
- Length of negotiation cycle
- Expansion conversations triggered by urgency framing

Use UTMs, lead-source tagging, and campaign IDs to isolate *urgency-driven behaviors.*

MONITOR SALES ACTIVITY AND BEHAVIOR

Urgency doesn't just move prospects. It changes how reps work. Watch for:

- Higher outreach velocity when urgency assets are introduced.
- More consistent messaging around pain, timelines, and consequence.
- Reduced "let me check back next quarter" cycles.
- Faster call-to-close times in urgency-sourced opportunities.
- Better executive alignment (e.g., more C-level meetings).

Bonus tactic: Run a split test with two sales teams—one using urgency plays, one using business as usual. Track:

- Win rate.
- Sales velocity.
- Deal size.
- Buyer engagement score.

Behavior proves belief. If reps adopt urgency-based frameworks, it means they're seeing it work. Don't forget to measure urgency's impact on cross-functional alignment. When urgency is well executed, you'll see faster collaboration between marketing and sales, tighter feedback loops with product, and increased customer service engagement during expansion and renewal cycles. Track internal KPIs like campaign response time, sales-enablement asset usage, and time from asset creation to field deployment. These reveal how deeply urgency is being operationalized—not just evangelized.

WATCH FOR EXECUTIVE INVOLVEMENT

Urgency doesn't just create more deals. It elevates deals. Track:

- Percentage of opportunities with executive sponsor involved before decision.
- Time from champion meeting to C-level alignment.
- Executive opens on ROI briefs or risk assessments.
- Number of Strategic Briefs downloaded or forwarded.
- Inbound messages from leadership (e.g., "Just saw this from my team—can we talk?").

When urgency hits the boardroom—that's when momentum becomes unstoppable.

QUANTIFY THE COST OF INACTION—IN REVERSE

Flip your cost-of-delay narrative inward.

Ask: "What was the financial impact of *not* using urgency before?"

Look at:

- Deals that stalled and never closed—could urgency have prevented it?
- Low-value renewals that weren't expanded.
- Missed cross-sell opportunities due to lack of timeline pressure.
- Product features underused because adoption wasn't accelerated.
- High-usage accounts that never made it to case study stage due to passive success motion.

This isn't just theory. You're building a *revenue case for making urgency a core competency.*

CONDUCT CUSTOMER WIN INTERVIEWS

Data is critical. But so is story. Ask customers:

- "What made you decide to act when you did?"
- "What would've happened if you waited another quarter?"
- "What was the moment this became urgent for you?"
- "What was happening inside your org that this helped solve immediately?"
- "Which content, message, or insight pushed you from interest to action?"

You'll discover:

- Which parts of your urgency story worked.
- Which stakeholders were most affected.
- What buyers saw as credible urgency (vs. gimmicks).

This helps you refine the play—and give your next prospects even more *proof.*

CREATE AN "URGENCY DASHBOARD" FOR LEADERSHIP

Present urgency as a measurable GTM discipline. Your dashboard should include the following metrics:

Metric	Before Urgency	After Urgency	Delta
Demo-to-close time	34 days	21 days	−38%
Win rate	22%	31%	+9 pts
Multi-threaded opps	38%	62%	+24 pts
Pipeline influenced by urgency content	—	$6.3M	—
Renewals with Strategic Briefs	12%	47%	+35 pts
Expansion from cost-of-delay reports	$0	$1.1M	+$1.1M

This is how you justify:

- Campaign continuation.
- Team expansion.
- Bigger budgets.
- More integration across the org.

Urgency stops being a *nice-to-have.* It becomes a revenue discipline.

REAL-WORLD EXAMPLE: SAAS HR PLATFORM TRACKS URGENCY ROI

A fast-scaling HR tech company knew it had a strong product—but deals often dragged. Their platform helped companies streamline hiring and reduce offer declines, yet many buyers treated the problem like a minor inconvenience, not a critical cost. So, the company launched a focused 60-day urgency campaign titled: "The Hidden Cost of Offer Declines."

The goal: Prove that slow decision-making and lack of urgency were hurting companies more than they realized—and show what happened when that urgency was created and tracked intentionally.

Here's what they did:

- *Built an "Offer Decline Cost Calculator"* that quantified how much revenue was lost due to slow hiring, delayed feedback, or counteroffers accepted elsewhere.
- *Published an executive benchmark report* showing how high-performing companies moved from offer to acceptance 2.4× faster—and retained talent longer as a result.
- *Enabled sales reps with urgency scorecards*, personalized to each buyer's time-to-hire metrics, showing how even a seven-day delay resulted in measurable revenue drag.
- *Embedded urgency-themed CTAs* in emails, demos, and proposals: "Every declined offer sets your Q3 behind by 2.6 weeks—here's how to fix that."

What they tracked and what happened:

- *Improved inbound response speed by 44%*—buyers replied faster when the cost of delay was front and center.
- *Demo-to-decision time dropped* from 29 days to 17—urgency shortened the sales cycle.
- *Stakeholder count per deal increased* from 2.1 to 3.6—urgency content pulled in HR, Finance, and even Sales Ops.
- *Win rate increased* from 24% to 36%—deals moved faster *and* closed at higher rates.
- *Expansion revenue within 30 days*—$640K directly tied to urgency-framed tools like pipeline risk visualizations and recruiting friction audits.
- *Executive opens of the benchmark report were 180% higher* than for their average content—it became the most forwarded document in two quarters.

Their conclusion?

"Urgency content didn't just drive clicks—it created a higher intent buyer profile. It reframed our solution as a 'right now' decision, not a roadmap item. It gave our reps the leverage they needed to move stalled conversations forward."

And they didn't stop there. The company reinvested. They turned the campaign into a permanent GTM motion, integrating urgency diagnostics into onboarding, and making benchmark data a standard part of sales follow-up. They didn't just create urgency—they measured its ROI. Then they scaled it. That's the playbook.

Action Checklist

- ☐ Benchmark pre-urgency metrics: sales cycle, win rate, decision speed, stakeholder engagement.
- ☐ Tag and track urgency-influenced campaigns across marketing and sales.
- ☐ Split-test urgency talk tracks or content with select sales teams.
- ☐ Monitor C-level involvement in urgency-driven opportunities.
- ☐ Reverse engineer missed deals to quantify the cost of passive GTM.
- ☐ Conduct customer win interviews to identify urgency triggers.
- ☐ Build a cross-functional dashboard to show leadership the impact.
- ☐ Position urgency not as creative—but as a growth strategy with ROI.

Chapter 39

TURNING CLICKS INTO ACTION—BUILDING URGENCY INTO YOUR WEBSITE

Your website is your first—and often only—chance to create urgency. It's the front line of your funnel. And yet most B2B websites are digital brochures: clean, polished, and completely forgettable.

They tell. They show. But they don't move people.

Here's what too many companies get wrong: They optimize for navigation, not conversion. They write for committees, not for urgency. And in doing so, they fail to answer the only question your buyer is really asking:

Why should I do something about this right now?

This chapter is about fixing that. Because in today's B2B environment, a website that doesn't create urgency doesn't create pipeline.

STOP EXPLAINING, START PRESSURIZING

The first mistake most companies make? They spend the top half of their homepage explaining what they do. But your buyer doesn't care—not yet.

Your hero section (the part visible on your homepage before scrolling) should be engineered to make them feel:

- The cost of doing nothing.
- The urgency of a problem they're currently ignoring.
- The fear that their competitors are solving this while they're sleeping on it.

Instead of: "We're the most advanced AI-driven analytics platform . . ."

Say: "You're losing 30% of revenue due to unmonitored blind spots—and don't even know it."

Urgency isn't about shouting. It's about creating an uncomfortable contrast between where the visitor is now and what happens if they stay there.

LEAD WITH THE PROBLEM— AND MAKE IT VISIBLE

Buyers don't act because you describe your product. They act because you show them a problem they can't ignore.

Use your homepage to surface that problem. Some ways to do that:

- Visuals that expose real consequences (e.g., charts, risk heat maps, checklist scores).
- Interactive elements: "Find out if you're at risk," "Run a quick self-assessment," "Get your score."
- Clear problem-first messaging: "Most teams fail to catch X—here's why it matters."

Make the invisible, visible. That's how you spark movement.

ADD FRICTION WHERE IT MATTERS MOST

This sounds counterintuitive, but urgency isn't always about removing friction. It's about strategic tension.

Use CTAs that introduce a risk or consequence:

- "See what you're missing."
- "Find your blind spots."
- "Calculate the cost of doing nothing."

These create micro-moments of discomfort—and prompt action. Instead of asking visitors to "Learn More," ask them to discover something about their current risk.

USE SOCIAL PROOF TO AMPLIFY FOMO

Nothing fuels urgency like proof that others are ahead of you.

Your site should showcase:

- Competitors or industry peers already solving the problem.
- Stats about adoption, time-to-value, or quantified wins.
- Testimonials that start with "Before we used this . . ."

Buyers don't want to be the first. But they also don't want to fall behind. Show them they already are.

BUILD CONVERSION PATHS THAT MATCH BUYER TENSION

Not every buyer is ready to talk to Sales. But most sites only offer two options: "Book a Demo" or bounce.

Instead, offer paths aligned to the buyer's urgency stage:

- No urgency: "Take the 2-minute risk assessment."
- Early urgency: "See how you compare to your peers."
- High urgency: "Talk to an expert today."

Meet buyers where they are—and give them just enough pressure to move one step further.

MAKE YOUR MESSAGING ABOUT INACTION, NOT JUST VALUE

Your entire site—not just the homepage—should communicate the consequences of inaction.

Ask:

- What does it cost the buyer to delay?
- What's happening while they're stuck in indecision?
- What's at stake if they don't fix this?

Great copywriting doesn't just communicate value. It confronts the reader with risk.

OPERATIONALIZE URGENCY WITH REAL-TIME SIGNALS

Use your martech stack to act on urgency:

- Trigger retargeting ads within hours of a key page visit.
- Send personalized emails based on behavioral indicators (e.g., high bounce rate from a product page = "Still figuring out how this impacts you?").
- Use chatbots to detect visitor type and serve urgency-based offers ("Want to see how exposed your system is?").

Your site should feel alive—not static.

TEST FOR ACTION, NOT JUST AESTHETICS

Too many website redesigns are judged by visual polish or internal stakeholder opinion.

Instead, ask:

- Does this page create discomfort around the problem?
- Does this CTA feel too easy—or just easy enough?
- Are we getting more qualified conversions from the visitors we want?

Urgency is not about beauty. It's about movement. Your website is not a museum. It's a battleground. Every visitor who leaves without acting is a lost opportunity. Not because they weren't interested—but because they didn't feel the need to act now. Fix that, and your website becomes your bestseller.

Action Checklist

- ☐ Rewrite your homepage headline to focus on a problem, not your product.
- ☐ Add a visual or interactive element that reveals risk or gaps.
- ☐ Replace soft CTAs ("Learn More") with pressurized language.
- ☐ Showcase peer proof to activate fear of falling behind.
- ☐ Create conversion paths for different urgency levels.
- ☐ Inject cost of inaction messaging throughout your copy.
- ☐ Use automation to follow up with urgency-specific messaging.
- ☐ Test and optimize based on conversion and discomfort, not just design.

Chapter 40

CREATING URGENCY IN PRODUCT-LED GROWTH AND SELF-SERVE MOTIONS

In product-led growth (PLG) and self-serve models, the buyer is in control. They:

- Sign up on their own.
- Onboard themselves.
- Explore when ready.
- Decide if and when to upgrade.

There's no SDR. No AE. No custom demo. So where does urgency come from? Right here: In PLG, the product *is* the salesperson—and urgency lives in the experience. This chapter gives you a blueprint to build urgency without a human touch and turn product curiosity into paid conversions—fast.

THE URGENCY CHALLENGE IN PLG

PLG users are:

- Casual.
- Distracted.
- Exploratory.
- Comparing tools.
- Moving at their own pace.
- Often evaluating three to five other options.

And unlike enterprise sales cycles, there's no friction holding them back—but also *no* pressure moving them forward. That's why urgency must be:

- Embedded.
- Contextual.
- Data driven.
- Emotionally triggering.
- Timed with precision.

Let's dive into how.

Step 1: Trigger Urgency at the First Sign of Activation

You only have a few minutes after signup before most users disappear forever.

The clock starts the moment they:

- Land in the app.
- Complete the first task.
- Reach an "aha!" moment.
- Invite their team.

Trigger urgency right then with:

- "You're 80% to your first win—complete it in under 3 minutes."
- "You've uncovered 3 risky gaps. Let's fix them before they cost you."

- "Unlock full visibility by connecting your [CRM, email, data] now."
- "Your risk score is high—here's what that means."
- "Your report is ready—view it before it expires."

The goal: Don't wait for them to explore. Drive a critical action early.

Step 2: Use Time-Sensitive Offers Inside the Product

Scarcity and deadlines work—even in product flows. Try:

- *Expiring upgrades*: "20% off annual plan—expires in 2 hours."
- *Time-boxed free trials*: "Upgrade by Friday to keep your data."
- *Progress-driven offers*: "Get access to advanced features for 7 days if you complete setup today."
- *Seat-based urgency*: "Add your team now and keep Starter Plan pricing—ends soon."

Visual cues matter:

- Countdown timers
- Badges
- Locked gates
- Animations tied to time or usage

Urgency must feel immediate, visual, and tied to real benefit.

Step 3: Build Urgency into Onboarding and Feature Activation

Each product milestone should unlock emotional momentum.

Examples:

- "You've set up your first rule—now let's automate 3× more tasks in 2 minutes."
- "You created your first dashboard. Want to benchmark it against your industry?"

- "Only 12% of users reach the ROI goal this fast—you're on track. Let's finish strong."
- "Don't lose this progress. Save your workflow and get a success score now."

Create a journey map that:

- Shows what's next.
- Surfaces the stakes.
- Quantifies value.
- Adds peer pressure or social proof.
- Highlights opportunity cost of not continuing.

You're not just onboarding. You're creating micro urgency loops.

Step 4: Send Behavior-Based Nudges Outside the Product

Email, in-app messaging, and push notifications should reflect:

- What they've done.
- What they haven't done.
- What they'll lose or gain by acting now.

Examples:

- "Your first report is waiting—it expires in 24 hours."
- "Users who do [X] in their first week are 3.5× more likely to succeed."
- "You haven't secured your setup—your data may be exposed."
- "Still on free plan? 82% of paid users activated premium features within 7 days."

Urgency messages work best when:

- They're triggered by behavior.
- They're personalized.

- They include why now matters.

Don't spam. Push with precision.

Step 5: Use Product Gating—but Tie It to Timing, Not Frustration

Free users expect limits. But don't just block features. Create *urgency-linked limits*:

- "You've hit your 3 free reports. Upgrade now to avoid data loss."
- "You're approaching your automation cap—act now to stay uninterrupted."
- "You've unlocked 2 of 5 insights—go Pro before they expire."
- "New insights are waiting—available for 48 hours only."

Gates shouldn't feel punitive. They should feel like natural forks in the road—with clear benefits for choosing speed.

Step 6: Create Urgency Moments Around Milestones

Celebrate momentum—and use it to push for the next step.

Examples:

- "Congrats! You completed 3 workflows in 1 day—let's supercharge automation."
- "You connected your data 4 days early—get 20% off our performance pack."
- "Your team hit 100 tasks. Now it's time to scale—here's how."

Use the following prompts:

- Pop-ups
- Modal windows
- Toast messages
- Follow-up emails
- In-app confetti + CTA

Momentum is emotional. Pair it with urgency-based action.

Step 7: Reinforce Urgency Through Data and Benchmarks

The best PLG tools mirror back performance—and use it to drive fear of falling behind. Add elements like:

- Industry benchmark comparisons.
- "Your performance vs. top 10%" reports.
- "Based on your team size, you're underusing key features."
- "Companies like yours automate 3× more by week 2."
- "You're leaving $4.8K/month in efficiency on the table—fix it now."

This isn't manipulation. It's reality, revealed through product insight. One overlooked but powerful tactic is to trigger urgency based on peer behavior. For example, when a similar company in the same industry upgrades or unlocks a feature, you can prompt the user with a statement like, "Teams like yours just adopted X—want to see what they're doing differently?" This builds social urgency without direct pressure and shifts the mindset from exploration to competitive awareness.

REAL-WORLD EXAMPLE: WORKFLOW SAAS CONVERTS 27% MORE WITH IN-PRODUCT URGENCY

A workflow automation platform noticed a frustrating pattern: Users were signing up for free trials but activating slowly—or worse, churning before reaching their "aha!" moment. Product adoption stalled in the first few days, and Sales never had a chance to intervene in time.

Instead of just adding more emails or improving help docs, the company redesigned the entire onboarding journey to infuse urgency directly inside the product.

Here's what changed:

- *"Quick Win Clock" on Day 1*: A visible countdown timer showed users how long it would take to fully automate their first workflow—emphasizing that value was just minutes away, not weeks.
- *Risk Score Alerts*: If a user hadn't connected key integrations within 72 hours, they saw a Risk Score pop-up: "Without your data flows active, you're losing 3.5 hours per week. Let's fix that now."
- *"3-Day Momentum Reward"*: Users who completed onboarding within three days received an exclusive 20% off upgrade offer. Framed as a reward—not a discount—it created a positive pressure loop.
- *Progress Bars + Deadline-Based Perks*: Each milestone showed a tangible outcome, paired with time-based nudges like "Unlock team analytics by Thursday—or lose visibility."
- *Email reinforcement*: Trial users received targeted nudges like, "This is your best 72-hour window to scale. Here's why our fastest-growing teams move now."

What happened?

- Trial-to-paid conversion increased by 27%. More users reached meaningful value—faster—and were willing to pay for it.
- Feature activation jumped 36% in the first 7 days. The onboarding design no longer waited for interest—it engineered momentum.
- Weekly active teams doubled. Instead of passive signups, they created users who acted—and stuck.

Why it worked: They didn't "sell harder." They made time and progress visible. By embedding urgency into the product experience—not just sales or marketing—they changed the psychology of adoption. The product became a race to results, not a sandbox to explore later. They turned onboarding from a passive experience into a ticking clock that rewarded action and revealed risk. And when urgency lives *inside* the product, conversion doesn't depend on a rep. It scales on its own.

Action Checklist

- ☐ Trigger urgency immediately after signup with next-step CTAs and time-limited nudges.
- ☐ Embed countdowns, offers, or limits into the onboarding journey.
- ☐ Tie feature access or success metrics to action within a time frame.
- ☐ Use behavior-triggered notifications to create personalized nudges.
- ☐ Gate usage in ways that encourage upgrade without frustrating users.
- ☐ Celebrate milestones and pair them with urgency-based CTAs.
- ☐ Surface performance gaps and peer comparisons to drive self-reflection.
- ☐ Design urgency loops as part of your PLG flow—not as afterthoughts.

Chapter 41

THE ROLE OF LEADERSHIP IN DRIVING A CULTURE OF URGENCY

Urgency is not a campaign. It's not just a sales playbook or a marketing tactic. Urgency is a culture—and culture comes from the top. If your leadership team doesn't model urgency, reinforce it, and demand it, then no amount of messaging, content, or tooling will make it stick. This chapter is about the the role of the CEO, the CRO, the CMO, and every other senior leader in creating a company that moves fast, acts decisively, and never waits for permission. Because urgency isn't something you ask for. It's something you demonstrate.

WHY URGENCY FAILS WITHOUT LEADERSHIP

You can teach reps how to push deals forward. You can show marketers how to spark intent. You can build urgency into your onboarding. But if leaders:

- Delay decisions
- Avoid conflict
- Tolerate slow performers
- Keep "waiting until next quarter"
- Fail to prioritize ruthlessly
- Reward caution over momentum

Then urgency becomes a theory—not a standard. Leadership is the lever of urgency.

MAKE SPEED A CORE VALUE—NOT A BUZZWORD

Fast companies win. They ship more. Learn faster. Close earlier. Iterate quicker. As a leader, you must define what speed looks like at your company:

- "We respond to qualified leads within five minutes."
- "We ship something valuable every two weeks."
- "We never let approvals delay execution more than 24 hours."
- "If you know something's broken, fix it—don't wait for permission."
- "We'd rather be 80% right today than 100% right too late."

Then *operationalize it* in the following functions:

- Onboarding
- Team meetings
- Performance reviews
- Goal setting
- How you make your own decisions

Culture doesn't form in slides. It forms in what gets rewarded. One of the most powerful ways leadership can reinforce urgency is through visibility—showing up where the work is happening. When a CEO joins a sales call, comments on a sprint board, or replies instantly to a blocker message in Slack, it sends a signal: What we're doing right now matters.

Speed isn't just expected—it's respected. It's a cultural cue that filters down to every team.

COMMUNICATE WITH INTENSITY—AND PRECISION

Leaders shape urgency with how they talk. Every word you use is a signal. Compare:

Passive Leadership	Urgent Leadership
"Let's circle back."	"Decide by EOD."
"We'll see how the market responds."	"Let's be first."
"I think we're in a good place."	"What's blocking us from launching now?"
"Maybe we can do this next quarter."	"Why not this week?"
"Keep me posted."	"Send me the result by Friday."

Speak like someone who believes that action now is better than perfection later. Your tone becomes your team's tempo.

ELIMINATE BOTTLENECKS—ESPECIALLY YOURSELF

One of the fastest ways leaders kill urgency is by being a bottleneck.

Examples:

- Approvals stuck in inboxes
- Legal or Finance delays

- Calendar congestion
- Constant "need more data" cycles
- Rewrites of already-approved plans

Fix this by:

- Delegating with authority.
- Setting response-time SLAs.
- Creating decision frameworks ("good enough to go").
- Blocking calendar time to unblock others.
- Empowering team leads to run sprints without full executive buy-in.

If you want speed, remove friction. Start with yourself.

MAKE URGENCY A HIRING STANDARD

You can't build a fast culture with slow hires. During interviews, screen for:

- Bias for action.
- History of fast learning and iteration.
- Clear decision-making.
- Stories of working under pressure.
- Disdain for bureaucracy.

Ask:

- "Tell me about a time you made a bold decision without perfect data."
- "What's your typical speed from idea to execution?"
- "When have you felt you moved too slow? What did you learn?"

Urgency isn't just a skill. It's a *disposition.* Hire for it.

EXPOSE THE COST OF INACTION—INTERNALLY

Make internal teams feel the pain of waiting. Use data to show:

- Pipeline lost from slow lead follow-up.
- Churn caused by passive renewals.
- Campaigns that launched too late.
- Products delayed and leapfrogged by competitors.
- Revenue missed due to indecision.

Say: "This isn't about moving faster for the sake of it. It's about what happens when we don't." Urgency becomes real when *you make the cost of inaction visible.*

MAKE "ACT NOW" THE DEFAULT OPERATING MODE

Urgent companies don't meet endlessly. They:

- Decide fast.
- Move fast.
- Learn fast.
- Fix fast.

Set these cultural norms:

- Default to action → launch MVP, then optimize.
- Challenge delays → "Is this truly a blocker?"
- Reward speed → celebrate those who create momentum.
- Build in short feedback loops → test weekly, not quarterly.
- Ship progress weekly → even if it's not perfect.

Leaders set the tone by:

- Making fast decisions in meetings.
- Letting go of perfect messaging or design.
- Pushing for timelines that feel uncomfortable—but doable.
- Saying: "Let's go."

PROTECT URGENCY FROM BURNOUT

Urgency isn't hustle porn. It's not panic. It's about *purposeful speed*, not constant chaos. You protect urgency by:

- Clarifying priorities (what matters *now*).
- Saying no to distractions.
- Giving teams the autonomy to run.
- Celebrating outcomes, not hours.
- Enforcing downtime after sprint cycles.
- Eliminating meetings and process bloat.

Urgency without clarity becomes anxiety. Urgency with alignment becomes momentum.

REAL-WORLD EXAMPLE: URGENCY CULTURE AT A HYPER-GROWTH SAAS COMPANY

At a 300-person SaaS startup with 3× growth, leadership embedded urgency by:

- Mandating all qualified inbound leads must be called within five minutes.
- Requiring weekly GTM syncs to ship *something* every seven days.
- Eliminating QBRs over 30 minutes.
- Creating a "Fastest Launch of the Week" award.
- Setting the company-wide mantra: "Speed Wins. Every Time."
- Having the CEO personally call back high-priority prospects when delays hit.
- Cutting 40% of internal meetings to create space for action.

Result?

- Shorter sales cycles
- Faster product adoption
- Clearer executive focus
- High-performance culture that didn't burn out—it bought in

They didn't just run fast. They made *urgency the operating system.*

Action Checklist

- ☐ Define speed and urgency as explicit company values with operating principles.
- ☐ Model urgent communication—short, specific, bold.
- ☐ Eliminate internal bottlenecks, especially in leadership approval flows.
- ☐ Hire for urgency: Seek people with a bias for action, ownership, and fast learning.
- ☐ Quantify and share the internal cost of delays and missed opportunities.
- ☐ Set team norms that favor quick execution over excessive planning.
- ☐ Build recovery and clarity into your culture to avoid burnout.
- ☐ Lead with urgency—not just in strategy, but in how you act every day.

Chapter 42

HOW TO KEEP URGENCY ALIVE AFTER THE CLOSE

Congratulations. The deal is done. The contract is signed. The sales team celebrates. Now what? If you're like most companies . . . the urgency disappears. Suddenly:

- Onboarding drags.
- Meetings get rescheduled.
- Customers go dark.
- Momentum fades.
- Expansion stalls.
- The value story loses power.

Why?

Because the muscle you built to create urgency pre-sale was never transitioned to post-sale. The best companies don't close urgency. They carry it forward. This chapter shows how to keep urgency alive long after the ink dries—so customers accelerate value, deepen usage, and become long-term champions.

TREAT THE FIRST 30 DAYS AS A "POST-SALE SPRINT"

Too many companies treat onboarding as a passive process. Checklists. Kick-off decks. Email reminders. Instead, launch a 30-day urgency sprint focused on three goals:

1. Time to first value
2. Executive validation
3. Proof that the pain is being solved

Frame it as:

- "We're moving fast because this is the most critical 30 days in our partnership."
- "Everything we do now sets the tone for ROI, expansion, and executive visibility."
- "Let's not slow down now—let's build on the momentum."

Speed keeps the emotional connection to the problem the company bought to solve.

RESET THE URGENCY NARRATIVE INTERNALLY

The prospect becomes a customer. But they also become a new buyer. And now, you have to sell them again. In your first customer-facing sessions:

- Revisit the pain.
- Quantify the cost of inaction.
- Recap the decision logic.
- Restate the transformation they committed to.
- Highlight the stakes and time sensitivity.

Example: "You bought to eliminate the $6.2M in IT ticket waste. We've designed this onboarding plan to get you 30% of that value in the first 30 days—and full value in 90." You're not just onboarding. You're reselling the reason they moved in the first place.

One simple way to reinforce urgency post-sale? Use the language of speed in every customer interaction. Swap "Let's discuss in a few weeks" with "Can we solve this in the next three days?" Replace "Let's see how it goes" with "What will success look like by Friday?" Language creates tempo. And the more your team speaks in timelines, the more your customers will operate with urgency.

CREATE AN URGENCY-BASED CUSTOMER SUCCESS PLAN

Every account should have a success plan built around urgency, not just usage.

Include:

- Key milestones with time frames.
- Executive update cadence.
- Adoption targets tied to outcomes.
- Risk thresholds (e.g., "If X isn't done by week 2, alert us").
- Expansion triggers ("Once Y team hits Z usage, we loop in procurement").
- A shared message, such as, "Here's what happens if we don't move fast—and how we'll avoid it."

Make it visual. Make it co-owned. Make it about business value, not task completion.

BUILD "FAST SUCCESS STORIES" IN THE FIRST 45 DAYS

Buyers don't just want progress. They want proof they made the right call. Design your onboarding to deliver a mini-win they can brag about:

- "We cut onboarding time by 37% in 3 weeks."
- "We replaced 4 legacy tools in 30 days."
- "We automated 22% of manual tasks before go-live."
- "Your team is using the platform 5× more than peer companies at this stage."

Give them:

- A metrics-based summary.
- A visual report.
- A story they can forward to the executive team.
- A CTA to expand, invite, or share with adjacent teams.

Fast proof builds trust. Fast trust builds urgency to grow.

USE EXECUTIVE CHECK-INS TO REINFORCE TIME-BASED VALUE

Executives disappear after the deal. Bring them back early and often.

Tactics:

- 30-day "ROI-in-motion" check-in
- 60-day "proof of momentum" deck
- Invite-only leadership webinar with early results
- Pre-renewal strategy session (scheduled on day one)

Position each as: "Here's how we're delivering what you paid for—ahead of schedule."

Make it:

- Visual.
- Business-outcome focused.
- Less than 15 minutes.
- Always tied to time.

Executives love progress. They move faster when they see acceleration.

USE THE PRODUCT TO KEEP THE STAKES VISIBLE

Inside the product, show:

- What's been achieved.
- What hasn't been touched.
- What's still costing them.
- What opportunities are waiting.

Examples:

- "You've automated 3 workflows—6 more identified, saving $9K/month."
- "Adoption in Team A is strong—Team B is falling behind."
- "Your compliance risk dropped 22%. Finish rollout to hit 80%."
- "You're still exposed in X area—fix it this week to stay audit-ready."

These aren't feature updates. They're *urgency updates*—tied to value, risk, and business goals.

CREATE EXPANSION MOMENTS EARLY—BUT AUTHENTICALLY

Don't wait for QBRs to talk expansion.

Instead:

- Trigger expansion conversations when success is proven.
- Use urgency-based language:
  - "You're about to hit capacity. Let's expand before usage slows."
  - "This other team is asking for access—want to bring them in now?"
  - "We have discounted bundles available until end of quarter."
- Present new problems: "You've solved X. Now here's the next threat you should tackle."
- Always tie back to timing: "If we start by [date], we'll have results before your board meeting."

Urgency isn't pressure. It's alignment around what's next.

RALLY INTERNAL TEAMS AROUND "POST-CLOSE URGENCY OWNERSHIP"

Sales owns the close. But Customer Service and Success and product teams must own the follow-through.

Make this clear in the following areas:

- Onboarding playbooks
- Weekly standups
- Comp plans (tie customer service bonuses to fast adoption or expansion)
- Success KPIs (time to first value, expansion by day 60, etc.)
- Leadership narratives

The message: "The sale starts when the contract is signed. Our job is to keep the urgency alive—because that's where the real value is delivered." When internal teams carry the baton, the customer never feels the energy drop.

REAL-WORLD EXAMPLE: SECURITY PLATFORM SCALES POST-CLOSE URGENCY

A fast-growing security platform with a strong PLG engine had no trouble driving inbound signups or free trials. But once deals closed, momentum stalled. Customers were slow to implement. Seat activation lagged. Expansion opportunities sat dormant.

The issue wasn't product-market fit. It was post-sale urgency. To fix it, the company reimagined onboarding—not as a support process, but as a high-stakes activation sprint.

Here's what they changed:

- *Reframed onboarding as a "Time-to-Protection Sprint"*: Instead of a generic implementation checklist, customers were told: "Our goal is to reduce your breach surface in 14 days. Here's how we'll do it."
- *Compressed go-live from 60 days to 14*: They mapped out the fastest path to meaningful protection, not full implementation. This created a sense of quick progress and built confidence.
- *Delivered a "Breach Risk Snapshot" within 48 hours*: A personalized report revealed three to five active misconfigurations or vulnerable access points—a wake-up call that made delay feel dangerous.
- *Scheduled a day-30 executive review with the customer's CISO or CTO*: The agenda? Quantify early impact, highlight future risks, and align on next steps—including expansion.

- *Highlighted unused protection areas in-app*: The dashboard called out "unsecured gaps" based on modules not yet deployed—encouraging customers to explore add-ons organically.
- *Triggered expansion outreach at 70% seat activation*: When usage crossed a certain threshold, Sales automatically offered scaled coverage options—tied to security KPIs, not just license limits.

Results:

- *38% increase in 60-day expansion*: Urgency didn't stop at close—it accelerated.
- *2× improvement in year-one retention*: Customers stuck around longer because they realized value sooner.
- *A customer satisfaction score on onboarding of 4.8*. What used to feel like handoff purgatory now felt like a milestone sprint.
- *Doubled executive engagement in six weeks*. CISOs and CTOs were pulled in early—not just for renewals, but for action.

Why it worked: They stopped treating "closed won" as the finish line—and treated it like the start of a new urgency arc. By giving onboarding a mission (protection, not setup), quantifying early risk, and keeping security leaders close, they created a psychological shift. Customers didn't feel like they were being managed—they felt like they were being secured.

This wasn't about "upsell pressure." It was about making urgency part of the experience—and making security progress too visible to ignore.

Action Checklist

- ☐ Run a post-sale sprint with onboarding, value realization, and fast proof.
- ☐ Reset the urgency narrative in the kickoff—restate the problem and why now matters.
- ☐ Co-create a success plan built around time-based milestones and risk.
- ☐ Deliver fast success stories within the first 30–45 days.
- ☐ Schedule executive check-ins with visible ROI and momentum updates.
- ☐ Use the product to highlight wins, gaps, risks, and expansion triggers.
- ☐ Initiate expansion conversations when urgency is real, not rehearsed.
- ☐ Make urgency post-sale a company-wide responsibility—not just that of customer service.

Chapter 43

URGENCY AS A COMPETITIVE ADVANTAGE

Most companies compete on:

- Features.
- Pricing.
- Integrations.
- Support.
- Brand equity.

But the companies that win repeatedly—even with inferior tech or smaller budgets—have one thing others don't: They make buyers act now. Urgency becomes a *competitive wedge.*

It compresses cycles. It blocks competitors. It influences budget timing. It elevates your message. It reshapes how buyers think—and how fast they move. In this chapter, we'll break down how to make urgency your unfair advantage.

THE PROBLEM WITH COMPETING ON CAPABILITY

When you sell features:

- Buyers compare.
- Analysts nitpick.
- Competitors copy.
- You enter price wars.
- Decisions get delayed.

Why? Because the buyer thinks, "We can decide next quarter. They'll still be here." But when you sell urgency? They think, "If we don't act now, we'll fall behind—and fast." That's how urgency shifts the battleground.

REDEFINE THE COMPETITION AS THE STATUS QUO

Most of your competitors aren't other vendors. They're:

- Inertia.
- Delay.
- Internal indecision.
- Manual work.
- Passive risk.
- Underperformance.

Urgency reframes the enemy. Say:

- "Your real competitor is inefficiency—and it's winning right now."
- "Doing nothing is the most expensive option."
- "Delay means decline—not stability."
- "The longer you wait, the more risk compounds."

Once buyers see inaction as the threat, you become the solution they can't postpone.

TRIGGER ACTION BEFORE YOUR COMPETITORS EVEN ARRIVE

When you control the timing, you control the deal. Ways to do it:

- Use early-stage tools (diagnostics, benchmark reports) to start the conversation first.
- Drop risk insights tied to regulatory, budgetary, or fiscal deadlines.
- Launch "health check" campaigns that surface immediate issues.
- Tie your offer to *this* quarter's priorities—not next year's wish list.

Say, "We're not asking for a roadmap discussion. We're showing you a risk that can't wait."

By opening the door early with urgency, you lock out the competition.

USE URGENCY TO REFRAME PRICE

Competitors may undercut you. But urgency reframes value. Say:

- "We're not the cheapest—but we'll deliver ROI in half the time."
- "Delaying for a lower price will cost more in lost revenue."
- "Price doesn't matter if the risk materializes first."
- "You'll spend more recovering from inaction than if you invest now."

Buyers often know what something costs. What they don't realize is what waiting costs. That's how urgency neutralizes discounting.

USE SPEED AS A SALES DIFFERENTIATOR

In fast-moving markets, speed isn't nice—it's necessary. Use these tactics:

- Commit to go-live timelines.
- Use rapid onboarding as a talking point.
- Highlight fast adoption from other customers.
- Share stories of same-week activation or ROI.
- Offer "quick start" bundles with guaranteed time-to-value.
- Make urgency your reputation: "They move fast and make it easy." Say: "We'll get you to value before [competitor] gets you a second demo."

Speed is a feature. Sell it. In competitive cycles, urgency is more than a tactic—it's a psychological edge. When buyers feel time pressure from one vendor and not the others, they unconsciously attribute higher credibility, confidence, and leadership to the one who's moving fast. They don't just think, "We need this now." They think, "These are the people who know what's coming next." That perception alone can shift the entire deal.

BUILD COMPETITIVE TOOLS THAT REVEAL RISK FASTER

Create assets your competitors can't match:

- Risk assessments
- Compliance scorecards
- Business case generators
- Cost-of-delay calculators
- Workflow audits
- AI-powered opportunity scans

Then say:

- "Here's what you didn't know."
- "Here's what it's costing you."
- "Here's why waiting even 30 days makes it worse."

The vendor that helps the buyer see the threat first wins the right to solve it.

TEACH YOUR TEAM TO SELL AGAINST "NEXT QUARTER"

The most common competitor? Not Vendor B. It's "Let's revisit in Q3." To avoid this, equip your GTM team with the following:

- Time-sensitive stories
- Objection busters tied to budget cycles
- End-of-quarter incentive plays
- Customer proof of what delays cost
- Real-world data tied to speed of adoption

Say: "The only reason to wait is if you think the problem will solve itself. Do you?" Make inaction feel irresponsible.

USE URGENCY IN COMPETITIVE BAKE-OFFS

Even in head-to-head deals, urgency wins. Tactics:

- Deliver a faster proof of concept.
- Highlight implementation risk from slower vendors.
- Provide a prebuilt business case that aligns to CFO expectations.
- Offer onboarding priority or team rollout support.
- Map your solution to board-level initiatives with a 30-day timeline.
- Emphasize your role as a partner in progress, not just a tech provider.

If all things are equal, buyers move with the vendor who says: "Here's how we start fast, deliver fast, and help you win faster."

REAL-WORLD EXAMPLE: MID-MARKET SAAS BEATS BIGGER RIVALS WITH URGENCY

A midsized observability platform repeatedly went head-to-head with industry giants like Datadog and Splunk—and won.

They didn't have more features. They didn't have a bigger brand. What they had was speed, simplicity, and urgency—and they made it their entire strategy.

Here's how they did it:

- *Deployed a "Three-Minute Stack Risk Scan" on the first call*: Instead of leading with a slide deck, they ran a quick diagnostic that exposed live misconfigurations in the buyer's environment. It wasn't a sales pitch. It was a wake-up call.
- *Promised full deployment in five business days*: While larger vendors talked about multiweek discovery and phased rollouts, this team committed to fast time-to-value—and backed it with real customer data.
- *Delivered executive dashboards by the end of week one*: This wasn't just a product promise. It was a credibility move. Decision-makers could see early value without needing to ask.
- *Armed sellers with stories of speed*: Reps consistently led with case studies like, "A Series C fintech firm replaced three tools and gained full-stack visibility in 10 days—all before their next board meeting."
- *Used pressure language without being pushy*: Their pitch wasn't "Buy now"—it was, "You can spend 3 weeks in discovery with the big guys . . . or we can have your execs seeing live performance insights by Friday."

The results?

- 23% higher win rate in competitive deals
- 30% shorter sales cycle
- 18% increase in average deal size

Why it worked: They didn't try to out-feature the incumbents. They out-executed them. They made urgency the differentiator—not just in their message, but in their experience.

Buyers didn't choose them because they had time. They chose them because they didn't. In a world where enterprise sales often drag and stall, this mid-market SaaS made the alternative feel faster, safer, and more decisive. They didn't just win deals. They moved the deal before the competition finished discovery.

Action Checklist

- ☐ Reframe the competition not just as other vendors, but as inertia.
- ☐ Launch early urgency plays to trigger engagement before rivals.
- ☐ Use urgency to shift focus away from price—and toward risk.
- ☐ Sell speed as a differentiator in messaging and proof.
- ☐ Arm GTM with tools that expose risk faster than competitors do.
- ☐ Train your team to sell against "next quarter" objections.
- ☐ In bake-offs, pair value with velocity to win decisions.
- ☐ Make urgency the reason you win—even when others match your tech.

Chapter 44

ACCELERATING ACTION WITH AI

How to Use Artificial Intelligence to Create Urgency

AI won't just change how we market and sell. It's already changing how urgency is created.

In today's attention-starved digital world, AI can give you superpowers—but only if you use it to reveal problems faster, personalize risk more accurately, and predict when your buyers are most ready to move. Here's the truth: Urgency that feels generic doesn't convert. But urgency that's personal, timely, and predictive? That changes everything.

This chapter shows how to use AI not to replace human connection, but to amplify the pressure to act.

USE PREDICTIVE INTENT SIGNALS TO SURFACE HIDDEN READINESS

AI tools can analyze web behavior, content consumption, and peer benchmarks to predict who's warming up—even before they raise their hand. If someone visits your product comparison page twice in one week, or starts consuming late-stage content, that's not a coincidence. It's a signal.

Use AI to:

- Identify micro-behaviors that suggest rising urgency.
- Score leads based on recency, frequency, and intent clusters.
- Automatically trigger tailored messages or SDR alerts to act while the window is open.

GENERATE URGENCY-FOCUSED MESSAGING ON THE FLY

AI copywriting tools can now write messaging at scale—but the magic isn't in automation. It's in contextual pressure.

Train your AI prompts to focus on:

- Cost of inaction for each persona.
- Emotional triggers by use case.
- Fear of falling behind versus the reward of solving now.

Then feed the AI:

- Risk signals.
- Industry benchmarks.
- Known customer pain points.

What comes out isn't just faster content—it's sharper, more urgent storytelling tailored to what the buyer is feeling now.

CREATE PERSONALIZED ASSESSMENTS AND REPORTS IN REAL TIME

Instead of sending static eBooks, use AI to build real-time, interactive experiences that:

- Ask questions.
- Score results.

- Show gaps.
- Recommend action.

These tools feel consultative—and the buyer generates the urgency themselves. It's not your pitch they trust. It's what they see in the mirror you held up.

USE AI TO SIMULATE THE COST OF DOING NOTHING

AI-powered ROI calculators can do more than justify spend. They can predict what happens if the buyer waits.

Build models that:

- Forecast security breach likelihood based on their configuration.
- Estimate revenue loss from underperformance.
- Visualize how delay compounds the problem.

When AI quantifies inaction, your story shifts from "what we offer" to "what you're risking."

FEED AI WITH REAL-TIME FEEDBACK TO TUNE URGENCY

AI isn't a one-way tool. It should learn what triggers work.

Set up systems where:

- Buyer response data (email opens, CTA clicks, form completions) feeds back into the messaging model.
- SDRs flag urgency objections ("It's not a priority") for tuning large language models and generating new prompts.
- Your urgency model gets smarter every week—and your messaging evolves dynamically.

USE AI TO COACH REPS ON URGENCY CONVERSATIONS

Tools like Gong and Chorus already use AI to analyze calls. Take it further:

- Flag missed urgency opportunities in discovery and demo calls.
- Score reps on their ability to surface pain and consequences.
- Generate follow-up scripts that introduce pressure where it was missing.

Now your reps aren't just informed—they're equipped to sell urgency better than ever. AI won't create urgency on its own. But it can remove the friction that stops humans from doing it well—the hesitation, the inconsistency, the lack of insight. Used right, AI lets you act faster, personalize better, and multiply the pressure to act across every buyer interaction. Urgency at scale—that's what AI makes possible.

Action Checklist

- ☐ Analyze behavior to predict buying intent and urgency windows.
- ☐ Use AI writing tools to generate pressure-driven messaging by persona.
- ☐ Create interactive tools and assessments that let buyers see their own risk.
- ☐ Build AI-powered ROI and inaction cost simulators.
- ☐ Feed real buyer behavior back into your models to sharpen urgency language.
- ☐ Use AI coaching tools to train reps to introduce urgency in every conversation.

Chapter 45

CREATING URGENCY AND CALM AT HOME

Most people think of urgency as a purely professional concept—the fuel that drives businesses to hit targets, outpace competitors, and seize opportunities. But urgency isn't confined to the office. In today's world, where work and home lives increasingly overlap, the ability to create urgency while preserving calm at home has become essential to success and sanity.

The truth is simple: If your home environment is chaotic, your sense of urgency collapses into stress. If your home is too relaxed, urgency disappears altogether, replaced by procrastination. The secret is striking the balance: cultivating urgency that motivates action and calm that sustains it.

WHY HOME MATTERS IN THE URGENCY EQUATION

When millions of people suddenly shifted to remote work, homes were forced to become offices, classrooms, gyms, and sanctuaries all at once. The boundaries blurred. Stress levels rose. Productivity often fell.

What many discovered is that urgency is not just about deadlines or KPIs—it's about the environment that either fuels action or smothers it. A cluttered home office, a disorganized daily rhythm, or a constant barrage of digital distractions all sabotage urgency. At the same time, too much pressure without space for recovery burns people out.

The home became the testing ground for whether urgency could be paired with calm. Those who succeeded found ways to build rituals, structure, and clarity that supported both.

PRINCIPLES FOR CREATING URGENCY AND CALM AT HOME

Design Your Environment for Momentum

Urgency at home begins with the physical space. Clutter signals indecision and slows momentum. Clear, simple, and purposeful environments signal action.

- Dedicate a consistent space for work.
- Reduce visible clutter to the essentials: tools you use daily.
- Keep cues of urgency (a whiteboard with priorities, a checklist, a visible timer) in sight, while keeping distractions (TV remote, non-work notifications) out of reach.

Urgency thrives in clarity. Calm emerges when you don't feel surrounded by noise.

Anchor the Day with Rituals

Rituals replace chaos with rhythm. A morning walk, a daily planning session, or even the act of shutting down your laptop at the same time each evening helps create urgency to start and calm to stop.

Think of rituals as psychological gear shifts:

- Morning: Create urgency with an activating ritual (exercise, writing your top three tasks).

- Midday: Restore calm with a pause (lunch without screens, five minutes of breathing, stepping outside).
- Evening: Reclaim calm with closure (review the day, plan tomorrow, then shut down).

Set Urgent, Not Overwhelming, Priorities

At work, endless to-do lists create anxiety. At home, they create paralysis. Instead, narrow your focus:

- Pick the *three outcomes that matter most today*.
- Break them into small, actionable steps.
- Make progress visible: Cross it off, check the box, highlight the win.

Urgency comes from clarity of what must be done now. Calm comes from knowing it's achievable.

Use Technology to Support, Not Sabotage

Working at home often means technology is both lifeline and distraction. Left unmanaged, it fuels stress and procrastination. Use it intentionally:

- Silence nonessential notifications.
- Time-box email and chat—urgency doesn't mean you respond instantly.
- Use focus tools (timers, "do not disturb" modes) to create momentum bursts.

Technology should amplify urgency, not scatter it.

Protect Recovery as Fiercely as Work

True urgency requires energy. Without recovery, energy fades and urgency turns into burnout. Calm at home is not indulgence—it's fuel.

- Schedule downtime with the same respect you schedule meetings.
- Protect sleep, exercise, and family meals as "nonnegotiables."
- Create device-free zones in the house.

Urgency and calm are not opposites. Recovery is the reset button that keeps urgency sustainable.

THE "URGENCY + CALM" HOME MODEL

Imagine your home life as two dials: urgency and calm. If urgency is high but calm is low, you get stress. If calm is high but urgency is low, you drift. The goal is high urgency and high calm: a home environment that sharpens focus while replenishing energy.

The formula is simple:

- Structure → Urgency
- Recovery → Calm
- Balance → Sustainable Momentum

Urgency at home doesn't mean living in constant stress. Calm at home doesn't mean slowing down. The power comes from combining both: urgency that drives you forward, and calm that allows you to sustain the pace. In a world where the lines between office and living room blur, those who master urgency and calm at home will not only thrive in their careers but also live richer, more fulfilling lives.

Action Checklist

- ☐ Clear your environment: Remove three things from your workspace that clutter or distract.
- ☐ Establish rituals: Choose one morning, midday, and evening habit that creates rhythm.
- ☐ Narrow priorities: Identify your top three outcomes for the day and track them visibly.
- ☐ Audit your tech: Shut off one nonessential stream of notifications this week.
- ☐ Protect recovery: Schedule a family meal, walk, or downtime block every day.

Chapter 46

YOUR FINAL ACTION CHECKLIST—EMBEDDING URGENCY EVERYWHERE

You've made it.

We've covered how to spark urgency in your messaging, product, pricing, campaigns, leadership, and culture. Now it's time to pull it all together. Because urgency isn't just a tactic. It's a repeatable system—one that belongs inside your GTM engine, not just your Q2 strategy deck.

This final chapter is your operational action checklist. Whether you're a CEO, CMO, CRO, product leader, or founder, these are the moves you can run again and again—to make your market move *now*.

SPARK THE FIRE: MAKE THE PROBLEM IMPOSSIBLE TO IGNORE

Lead with the problem. But not just any problem—the one your buyer doesn't yet realize they have.

- Use scans, diagnostics, benchmarks, and tools.
- Quantify hidden risk, inefficiency, or missed revenue.
- Visualize the cost of inaction.
- Reveal what's changing in the market—and why delay is dangerous.
- Anchor urgency in *today's* reality.

Urgency doesn't come from hype. It comes from truth, revealed.

PERSONALIZE THE STAKES FOR EVERY BUYER

No matter how good your campaign is, urgency dies when it's not tailored.

- Map your message to each stakeholder.
- Show each person their own risk and their own upside.
- Deliver briefings, dashboards, or playbooks by role.
- Use industry-specific data, benchmarks, or threats.
- Make the consequence personal—not theoretical.

If they don't see themselves in the problem, they won't act. Urgency multiplies when stakeholders feel the internal pressure to act before their peers. Equip your champions with assets they can use to drive urgency across the buying group—not just upward, but sideways and downward. Give them the visuals, metrics, and "what happens if we wait" scenarios that spark action in meetings you'll never attend. The more people who feel the clock ticking, the harder it becomes to delay.

BUILD URGENCY INTO THE PRODUCT AND EXPERIENCE

Your product must reinforce the message. Every touchpoint is a chance to remind users:

- What still isn't working.
- What they haven't yet unlocked.
- Where their exposure lies.
- What they could accomplish if they moved faster.
- What their peers are already doing.

Design urgency into the following:

- Onboarding
- Dashboards
- Nudges
- Gated features
- Expiring insights
- Progress timelines

This makes the product the pressure.

STRUCTURE OFFERS AND PRICING TO ACCELERATE ACTION

Don't leave your best growth lever on the table.

- Time-box incentives and bundles.
- Use pilot programs and fast starts to de-risk the leap.
- Make expansion cheaper *now* than later.
- Set pricing locks, implementation schedules, and success guarantees.
- Show what delays will cost—and why action this quarter matters.

Deadlines drive decisions. Create them—credibly.

TURN LEADERSHIP INTO A FORCE MULTIPLIER

Companies move at the speed of their leaders.

- Model decisive action.
- Speak with urgency.
- Celebrate speed and learning—not just results.
- Make "act now" the cultural default.
- Eliminate friction and slow hires.
- Reinforce the urgency narrative weekly.

If leadership isn't urgent, nothing else will be. You can't scale urgency without accountability. Bake it into KPIs. Track how fast teams respond to leads, how quickly blockers are resolved, and how long it takes to go from insight to action. Make speed a visible metric—on dashboards, in meetings, and in performance reviews. When everyone knows that urgency isn't just encouraged but expected, behavior changes.

AFTER THE DEAL CLOSES, NEVER LET URGENCY FADE

Urgency doesn't end with the signature. It begins there. To keep urgency high:

- Build fast wins into onboarding.
- Schedule executive updates with outcomes, not features.
- Highlight progress gaps in product dashboards.
- Use milestones to drive expansion.
- Treat success and adoption like a sales motion—not a support motion.

The companies that grow fast? They never stop selling the reason for urgency.

Conclusion

THE COMPANIES THAT WIN, MOVE FASTER

We live in a world of noise. Buyers are flooded. Teams are stretched. Everyone's busy. What gets attention now? The risk that feels immediate. The story that feels personal. The product that feels essential. The vendor that says, "Let's go now."

This book wasn't about pressure tactics. It was about clarity—and creating the conditions for action. Urgency doesn't come from louder marketing; it comes from tighter alignment—between the problem you solve, the value you deliver, and the moment your buyer is living through right now. If there's no tension, there's no movement. If there's no trigger, there's no decision. And that's why the companies that create urgency win—because they connect to what's already pressing on their buyer's world. Because when buyers see the truth—the risk, the inefficiency, the wasted time—and they trust that you can solve their unique problem?

They move. They buy. They expand. They advocate. That's how you go from pipeline . . . to revenue . . . to category leadership.

WHERE TO START: QUICK WINS THAT DRIVE URGENCY NOW

If you're ready to apply what you've learned, don't try to do everything at once. Start where urgency matters most—at the point where you're losing momentum today.

Here are six high-leverage moves to get fast traction.

1. Run a "Cost of Inaction" Workshop

Quantify the real cost of doing nothing—across pipeline, churn, and inefficiency. Use it to align your leadership team around urgency as a growth lever.

2. Rewrite Your Homepage Headline

Make it urgent. Make it about a problem. Make it impossible to ignore. You don't need a full rebrand—just one bold message that says, "We solve what can't wait."

3. Create a Risk or Benchmark Diagnostic Tool

Help buyers discover the problem for themselves. Give them a free scan, scorecard, or assessment that visualizes the risk of waiting.

4. Inject Urgency into Sales Conversations

Arm your team with a "Cost of Delay" calculator and new talk tracks that reframe the stakes. Show them how to shift the conversation from features to risks.

5. Launch a 90-Day Urgency Sprint

Pick one urgent narrative. Build cross-functional alignment. Flood the market with it. Make buyers act—before your competitors do.

6. Build a Slide Your Buyer Can Use Internally

Create one visual that shows the risk, cost, and impact of doing nothing—then hand it to your champion. When urgency becomes their story, deals move without resistance.

Start there. Move fast. Measure results. Then expand. Because urgency isn't a campaign—it's a discipline. And the companies that master it don't just grow. They become impossible to ignore.

ACKNOWLEDGMENTS

To my family, thank you for standing with me every step of the way.

Thank you to BenBella Books for making this book possible, and to Linda Konner for believing in it early and guiding it all the way through.

ABOUT THE AUTHOR

Steven Mark Kahan is a board advisor, CMO, go-to-market strategist, and serial entrepreneur who has helped grow seven startup companies from early stage to successful exits, generating over $5 billion in shareholder value.

He is the *Wall Street Journal*–bestselling author of *High-Velocity Digital Marketing* and a recognized voice on how to break through the noise, simplify complex products, and generate urgency that converts into revenue.

Steven is known for turning marketing from a cost center into a revenue engine—and helping companies outperform giants with speed, clarity, and execution. He advises tech companies across cybersecurity, SaaS, AI, and cloud industries, bringing decades of practical experience to the most important challenge every business faces: "How do we make buyers act now?"

He lives in Texas with his wife, Terry, and their family, and when he's not scaling companies, you'll find him writing, mentoring, or enjoying life with those he loves most.